At a time when much of what passes for feminism is actually a neo-liberal approach that privileges individual empowerment over revolutionary social change, Robert Jensen comes out with a much-needed book that is bound to put the radical back in feminism. His insightful analysis, unflinching commitment to radical feminism, and his courageous call to eradicate patriarchy makes *The End of Patriarchy: Radical Feminism for Men* a refreshing and bold text.

> — Gail Dines, Professor of Sociology and Women's Studies, Wheelock College, and author of *Pornland: How Porn has Hijacked our Sexuality*

This is a terrific, powerful, informative book. There is not one page without an idea worth discussing and exploring. Jensen emerges as a wise and humble man willing to listen to women and to question men. Such men are rare. He does the opposite of mansplaining: man-listening-to-women! I love it!

> — Jeffrey Masson, author of *Beasts: What Animals Can Teach Us About the Origins of Good and Evil*

Jensen presents a brilliant and brave analysis of patriarchy and its costs. His thoughts concerning rape, pornography, and transgenderism are deeply insightful and important—and especially compelling in their clarity and honesty. This book is a must-read for men and women who, like Jensen, care passionately about imagining and creating a sustainable, humane, and socially just world.

> — Rebecca Bigler, Professor of Psychology and Women's and Gender Studies, University of Texas

The End of Patriarchy is a must-read book for men—and women—who know in their gut that men's economic, social and political dominance does terrible harm to women *and* men, but who lack the cogent arguments or words to express how. With his trademark style that manages to convey both heartfelt humility and breathtaking moral clarity, Robert Jensen expresses the fear that so many men have of engaging deeply with feminist ideas— as well as the incalculable rewards for those willing to take the leap.

> — Jackson Katz, PhD, author of *The Macho Paradox: Why Some Men Hurt Women*

Women will be grateful for this book because Robert Jensen will be heard by men in a way that women are not. If men will open their minds to it, it will change their lives.

> — Betty McLellan, PhD, author of *Unspeak A feminist ethic of speech.*

T0163221

Read this book. Reckon with it. In a culmination of his life's work to understand, address, and resist inequality, Robert Jensen offers us a critical interrogation of patriarchy and male dominance and also a call to action. This book is important and uncomfortable, and it is both of these things because of Jensen's unflinching radical analysis and deep emotional honesty.

— Matthew B. Ezzell, PhD, Associate Professor of Sociology,
James Madison University

In *The End of Patriarchy*, Robert Jensen reveals that far from being an outmoded ideology, radical feminist thought is a political practice that transforms us from the inside out forcing us to confront the painful and profound ways in which patriarchy distorts our collective humanity. He challenges all of us to reconsider how radical feminism can help us to think through the most pressing social issues of the current moment from the persistence of rape culture to patterns of ecological destruction that threaten the future of human life on the planet. This book is an invitation to engage with radical feminism's insights and the critical strategies for imagining a better and more just social order. A truly powerful and necessary text.

— Courtney Morris, Assistant Professor,
The Pennsylvania State University

For more than two decades Robert Jensen has been a thorn in the side of patriarchy, pushing us to see how a sexist world both constructs and constrains who we are. He simultaneously dares us to look inside at the damage it's done to us, and to imagine a world beyond its cruel constructs. I don't always agree with him, but I believe it is imperative that I read his work, wrestle with his ideas. Some of his ideas are not 'nice' but they are necessary.

— Michael Kimmel, Distinguished Professor of Sociology,
Stony Brook University, and author of *Angry White Men*

To end patriarchy, men must confront male domination and stop it. That might seem like too tall of an order, but in *The End of Patriarchy* Robert Jensen turns that personal challenge into a political call to action. He daringly shows that radical feminist thought and action is essential to our survival as a species and planet. Through his self-reflection and critical thinking, we discover a man who is a role model for men and boys, students and activists, in the struggle to create a genuine society free from misogyny and inequality.

— Kathleen Barry, Professor Emerita, author of *The Prostitution of Sexuality* and *Unmaking War, Remaking Men*

Patriarchy is the water that we swim in, and it is poisonous and rank. Unless we see that, how can we ever escape into fresh clean air? In this lucid, balanced and immaculately argued book, Robert Jensen builds his case inexorably towards answering the biggest questions of our lives. Can we re-discover an equal society for humans? Can we live on this earth? We did once, and we can again. This is a book of hope.

— Steve Biddulph AM, author of *The New Manhood*

Drawing on his many years of work, challenging toxic masculinity and the 'pathology of patriarchy', Robert Jensen shows what it really means—in both political and deeply personal ways—for men to support an end to systems of male dominance. Any man who considers himself an ally of the feminist movement should read this book. And then they should encourage every man they know to read it too.

— Meagan Tyler, PhD, Vice-Chancellor's Research Fellow,
RMIT University, and co-editor of *Freedom Fallacy:
The limits of liberal feminism.*

The End of Patriarchy poses a bold challenge to both the patriarchal inequalities which brutalise women and limit men and the stunted visions of gender and its transformation visible in contemporary gender politics. In this highly readable and passionate work, Robert Jensen offers an eloquent account of the implications of radical feminist insights for men's everyday lives and choices.

— Michael Flood, PhD, Associate Professor,
University of Wollongong

At a point where women's betrayal by the male left has been near-universal, Robert Jensen does a service to feminism in recognising that the best hope for the planet lies in radical feminist thinking and action.

— Julia Long, PhD, lecturer and lesbian feminist activist, author of
Anti-Porn: The Resurgence of Anti-Pornography Feminism

Photo credit: Nerissa Escanlar

Robert Jensen is a professor in the School of Journalism at the University of Texas at Austin, where he teaches courses in media law, ethics, and politics and is a Regents' Outstanding Teaching Award winner. Jensen is a board member of Culture Reframed and the Third Coast Activist Resource Center.

Other books by Robert Jensen

Plain Radical: Living, Loving, and Learning to Leave the Planet Gracefully (2015)

Arguing for Our Lives: A User's Guide to Constructive Dialog (2013)

We Are All Apocalyptic Now: On the Responsibilities of Teaching, Preaching, Reporting, Writing, and Speaking Out (2013)

La Angustia en el Sueño Americano/The Anguish in the American Dream (Translated by Mariano Hernan Spina, 2013)

All My Bones Shake: Seeking a Progressive Path to the Prophetic Voice (2009)

Getting Off: Pornography and the End of Masculinity (2007)

The Heart of Whiteness: Confronting Race, Racism and White Privilege (2005)

Citizens of the Empire: The Struggle to Claim Our Humanity (2004)

Ciudadanos del Imperio: Reflexiones sobre patriotismos, disidencias y esperanzas (2003)

Writing Dissent: Taking Radical Ideas from the Margins to the Mainstream (2001)

Pornography: The Production and Consumption of Inequality (with Gail Dines and Ann Russo, 1998)

Freeing the First Amendment: Critical Perspectives on Freedom of Expression (co-editor with David S. Allen, 1995)

THE END OF PATRIARCHY

Radical Feminism for Men

ROBERT JENSEN

First published by Spinifex Press, 2017

Spinifex Press Pty Ltd
PO Box 212
North Melbourne, Victoria, 3051
Australia
women@spinifexpress.com.au
www.spinifexpress.com.au

Edited by Renate Klein, Pauline Hopkins and Susan Hawthorne
Typeset by Blue Wren Books
Cover Design by Deb Snibson
Indexed by Karen Gillen
Typeset in Minion Pro
Printed in the United States

National Library of Australia Cataloguing-in-Publication data:
Jensen, Robert, 1958– author.
The end of patriarchy: radical feminism for men / Robert Jensen; afterword by Rebecca Whisnant.

9781742199924 (paperback)
9781742199894 (ebook : epub)
9781742199870 (ebook : pdf)
9781742199887 (ebook : mobi)

Includes bibliographical references and index.

Patriarchy
Feminism
Gender identity
Sex differences

Other Creators/Contributors:
Whisnant, Rebecca, writer of Afterword.

305.3

CONTENTS

ACKNOWLEDGEMENTS

Thanks to the network of friends who have connected through our shared affection for the late Jim Koplin.

Thanks to Gail Dines, Matt Ezzell, and Rebecca Whisnant for many years of feminist solidarity.

Thanks to Peter Dimock, Nancy Gilkyson, Carla Golden, Heather McLeod, Tai Moses, and Pat Youngblood for critical readings.

Thanks to Eliza Gilkyson for being my touchstone.

And special thanks to Susan Hawthorne, Pauline Hopkins, and Renate Klein at Spinifex Press, not only for their generosity to me in our work on this book but for a quarter century of exemplary efforts in support of feminist scholarship and organizing.

In *Getting Off: Pornography and the End of Masculinity,* published by South End Press in 2007, I explored some of the same themes found here. When South End went out of business in 2014, *Getting Off* went out of print. *The End of Patriarchy* expands on that work, going beyond pornography, with a more comprehensive feminist framework and additional topics.

Some of the ideas in *The End of Patriarchy* were first expressed in essays published in edited volumes, newspapers, magazines, and websites, including:

"Pornographic Values: Hierarchy and Hubris," *Sexualization, Media, and Society,* 1:1 (2016): 1–5.

"Letting Go of Normal when 'Normal' Is Pathological, or Why Feminism Is a Gift to Men," in Donna King and Catherine G. Valentine, eds., *Letting Go: Feminist and Social Justice Insights and Activism* (Nashville, TN: Vanderbilt University Press, 2015), pp. 57–65.

"Pornographic and Pornified: Feminist and Ecological Understandings of Sexually Explicit Media," in Jacob Held and Lindsay Coleman, eds., *The Philosophy of Pornography: Contemporary Perspectives* (Lanham, MD: Rowman & Littlefield/ Scarecrow Press, 2014), pp. 53–70.

"Stories of a Rape Culture: Pornography as Propaganda," in Melinda Tankard Reist and Abigail Bray, eds., *Big Porn Inc: Exposing the Harms of the Global Pornography Industry* (North Melbourne, Australia: Spinifex Press, 2011), pp. 25–33.

"Pornography," with Ana J. Bridges, in Claire M. Renzetti, Jeff Edleson, and Raquel Kennedy Bergen, eds., *Sourcebook on Violence Against Women* (Thousand Oaks, CA: Sage, 2011, 2nd ed.), pp. 133–149.

"Pornography Is What the End of the World Looks Like," in Karen Boyle, ed., *Everyday Pornography* (New York: Routledge, 2010), pp. 105–113.

"Is the ideology of the transgender movement open to debate?" *Voice Male*, Summer 2016; and *Feminist Current*, June 27, 2016. <http://www.feministcurrent.com/2016/06/27/ideology-transgender-movement-open-debate/>

"How porn makes inequality sexually arousing," *Washington Post*, In Theory, May 25, 2016. <https://www.washingtonpost.com/news/in-theory/wp/2016/05/25/how-porn-makes-inequality-sexually-arousing/>

"Can porn be good for us?" *The Economist*, November 17–27, 2015. <http://debates.economist.com/debate/online-pornography?state=closing>

"Feminism unheeded," *Nation of Change*, January 8, 2015. <http://www.nationofchange.org/2015/01/08/feminism-unheeded/>

"Rape, rape culture, and the problem of patriarchy," *Waging Nonviolence*, April 29, 2014. <http://wagingnonviolence.org/feature/rape-rape-culture-problem-patriarchy/>

"Rape is all too normal," *Dallas Morning News*, January 20, 2013. <http://www.dallasnews.com/opinion/sunday-commentary/20130118-robert-jensen-rape-is-all-too-normal.ece>

BEGIN IN THE BODY

This book began in my body.

I first encountered a radical feminist analysis of patriarchy at the age of thirty when I showed up for graduate school, sat down in a course on freedom of expression and the law, and stumbled upon an article that presented a feminist critique of pornography. My initial reaction was that such a critique was absolutely ridiculous, while at the same time recognizing that it was undeniably true.

It's not surprising that I was a bit conflicted. As a man with years of socialization into patriarchal masculinity behind me, I was wary of feminists, who I had been told were out to get me. If a feminist critique of anything seemed compelling at first, I had an incentive to eliminate the threat—explain why it must be wrong and move on. But even though I had been trained to reject such ideas, at a deeper level I felt a sense of relief, a recognition that I was reading not only an honest account of the world but of myself, a coherent explanation of my own experience that I had no words for at that moment.

Despite that resonance, as I read more about the critique of pornography and feminism generally, I intensified my skepticism and evaluated the arguments with all the scholarly rigor of a budding academic—identifying assumptions, questioning definitions, evaluating evidence, challenging claims. Such skepticism is appropriate in examining any argument that anyone makes about anything, but skepticism that masks fear can lead us to caricature ideas that feel threatening, and my first attempts at writing about the feminist challenge to men's use of pornography did just that. Luckily, my body wouldn't allow me to take the cheap way out.

I first approached feminism through this intellectual work, keeping my distance. But in ways that I could not have articulated in that moment, I was also being pulled into feminist analysis and politics by my body—something just felt right about the critique of patriarchy. We may like to tell neat, tidy stories about how we come to believe what we believe—tales in which we usually are the critical-thinking heroes—but the way all of us come to understand the world involves the complex interaction of emotion and reason, body and mind, conscious mental activity and unconscious body memory. We 'think' and we 'feel' at the same time, intertwined, even though we often talk as if those two words mark wholly separate activities in walled-off compartments of our brains and bodies.

This doesn't mean we shouldn't think critically, or that an intellectual argument can be defended simply by describing a feeling. In this book I offer an argument for a feminist critique of patriarchy that I believe is based on the rigorous use of reason, and readers should critique my assumptions, definitions, evidence, and claims. But we need not sacrifice rigor to pay attention to our emotional, embodied life and what it teaches us.

As I try to make sense of how this thinking-and-feeling about the sex/gender system unfolded in my life, it's clear that the story is not neat or tidy and that I am not particularly heroic. Even though I wanted to reject the feminist critique, my body was telling me not to turn away, even when this challenge to patriarchy would demand critical self-reflection that was painful. However intense that pain, it would be worth it. Something in me—call it instinct, or inspiration, or dumb luck—kept me reading and thinking. I remained skeptical but with an increasingly open mind.

So, I could concoct a story about how I embraced radical feminism as a result of a careful intellectual process—how a purely rational evaluation of the analytic power of feminist theory led me to accept a compelling argument for a feminist politics rooted in our shared moral commitment to human dignity, solidarity, and equality. Feminist theory offers such an analysis and feminist politics is compelling, but the more accurate story is that I first embraced feminism out of self-interest, out of a desire for something more in life than what patriarchy offers men. I wanted out of the endless competition to 'be a man' as defined by patriarchy and was looking for a way simply to be the human being I imagined I could be. Through feminism, I came to understand that the fear and isolation I felt, and many men feel, was the result of a conception of masculinity in patriarchy that traps us in an endless struggle for control, domination, and conquest. The problem was not my failure to live up to the standards of masculinity but the toxic nature of masculinity in patriarchy. And through feminism, I came to understand that the way I was used as a child by other boys and adults wasn't the result of my weakness or failure but was the product of patriarchy's brutal sex/gender system that sexualizes domination and subordination.

I also came to understand that patriarchy had not only constrained my life and left me vulnerable when I was young, but trained me to embrace that domination/subordination dynamic as I got older. I may never have felt 'man enough', but eventually I learned enough to act out some of those toxic masculinity norms in ways I was not proud of. We want to understand how we have been hurt, but unless we are sociopaths we also have a moral yearning to understand how and why we have hurt others. Feminism provided a framework to understand the injuries I had endured and the injuries I had inflicted, by explaining how patriarchy's imposition of a sex/gender hierarchy was one of the key forces that structured the world in which I lived, a world I wanted to understand more clearly and help change.

That story is more accurate, but still too neat and tidy, sounding too much like one of those 'journey narratives' in which the hero moves through challenges and braves obstacles to enlightenment. But even when we learn to analyze patriarchy, we still live in patriarchy and face the endless challenges that it presents, complicated even further by the other toxic systems of power that structure the world: white supremacy, capitalism, First World domination, and human arrogance in the larger living world. The more we sharpen our capacity to understand, the more we are able to see our failures.

And through it all we analyze and critique, not as free-floating minds, but as embodied creatures. We think and feel our way through this multifaceted world, using not only our intellectual tools but all of our capacities to understand that complexity the best we can. If we are lucky, we have moments of clarity along the way, but if we are honest we never stop struggling to deepen our understanding.

This book began in my body and I begin this book with that recognition because I know that I am not alone in this experience. While working on this book I received an email from a woman who had read some of my writing on pornography and sent me questions regarding her ongoing research on violence. But before raising those issues, she told me a bit of her story, which she gave me permission to share here. It is a story both unique in its specific trajectory while at the same time commonplace, a reminder of Muriel Rukeyser's insight: "What would happen if one woman told the truth about her life? The world would split open."[1]

Lisa, a woman in her 30s today, told me this about her world:

> Throughout my 20s I thought that I was a normal person. I lived and worked and dated, and I was ok. I was also a person with growing insomnia, an increasing love for substances that could put me to sleep, a disappearing attention span, and a lot of eerie, confusing dreams. I started keeping a journal on nights when I couldn't sleep. A lot of it was incoherent. Almost all of it was about sex.
>
> By my early 30s sleeplessness, alcohol, and difficulty concentrating were reaching their limit. Unlike in my 20s, anything related to sex—scenes in movies, jokes among friends, sex itself—made me so inexplicably upset that I started to avoid them at all cost. They would give me insomnia for days and weeks, a kind of open-ended insomnia that I couldn't see the end of.
>
> That's when I saw a therapist for the first time, and over the course of the next several months a long stream of sexual encounters that I had never described in detail to anyone, that had happened with different people over the course of a decade, that I had always remembered and never forgotten, that had lived in my memories as wordless vignettes, that I had simply

---

1   Muriel Rukeyser, *Houdini: A Musical* (Ashfield, MA: Paris Press, 2002), p. 89.

assumed were normal but also always known were toxic, started to unravel.

When it was over, I looked at the wreckage and I wondered, how did this happen? How did I nearly die by allowing men to use my body? How could the damage accumulate so much without anyone noticing? I have so much more to offer the world, and I deserve so much more from the world than this.

Therapy saved my life, but looking a cruel and common sexual selfishness in the face while standing in front of its effects made me suddenly at odds with everyone. I'm at odds with people my age, I'm at odds with the movies, I'm at odds with advertisements, I'm at odds with dating websites. Healing myself and daring to ask questions turned out to be the loneliest thing I ever did.

I wanted to look to feminism for answers because I needed to understand, but I was shocked, literally traumatized again, by a brain-puzzle of empowerment and choice rhetoric [common in some contemporary feminist writing] that I can only describe as extremely painful for someone like me to read. I didn't choose any of this.

Throughout, no one had ever described radical feminist ideas to me, and so when I first found them it was like a small stream of fresh air found its way through a mostly closed window into a room with nearly no oxygen left. I don't need many people to agree with me, but I do need to know that I'm not completely alone.

I have a lot of ideas about the links between a culture of sexual selfishness and sexual violence itself. I know how it goes from liberated pop fantasy to a real person's body. I think that I'm not alone. I think that there are probably a lot of me.

Lisa's experience is not idiosyncratic, nor is her concern that some contemporary feminist analyses sidestep a radical critique of patriarchy and instead focus on ways in which women's choices within patriarchy can be 'empowering' for individual women. As it did for me, radical feminism helped Lisa bring the intellectual and the embodied together. Though her experience as a woman is dramatically different than mine as a man—I can take seriously my own pain without asserting a false equivalency with the threats that women face and the injuries they experience—in her story I recognized the world in which both she and I live.

My hope is that this book contributes to an understanding of the world that helps us deal with our individual pain and understand the system out of which that pain emerges. Central to that task, as Lisa makes clear, is facing our fears.

FOLLOW
YOUR FEAR

The advice of this age, routinely dispensed to people making major life and career choices, is 'pursue your passion'. There's no harm in that cliché if it's meant to encourage people not to accept spirit-crushing jobs for the sake of material comfort, or to remind us to speak our minds when people around us disagree. But in a society facing multiple, cascading social and ecological crises, the obsession with pursuing passions can be a dangerous diversion when those passions lead us to ignore painful realities. The more important advice—for all of us, individually and collectively—is first to 'follow your fears'.

If there is to be a decent human future on a robust living planet, we are going to have to confront our deepest fears, not only about ourselves but about the profoundly unjust and fundamentally unsustainable societies we have created. The problems we face are the predictable outcome of the social, political, and economic systems on which our societies operate and the underlying ideas that animate those systems. While it's true enough that the people running those systems are often greedy, sometimes incompetent, and occasionally cruel, our primary problem is not the nature of the people in charge but the nature of the systems they are in charge of.

In polite company we rarely speak of these systems directly, and when we do we often avoid naming and describing them accurately. In the United States it's common to hear people speak in favor of diversity but rarely do we confront the pathology of white supremacy, the ideology that Europeans created and used to justify their conquest of most of the world for 500 years. Even with the significant achievements of civil rights movements, this culture struggles to face honestly the effects of an enduring white supremacy that we claim we want to transcend.

The pathological greed that drove that conquest eventually developed into contemporary corporate capitalism, with its demand for endless growth and its inevitable wealth inequality. Yet rather than rejecting an economic system that is at odds with our own basic moral principles and with an ecologically viable future, we pretend that superficial reforms sold with terms such as 'conscious capitalism' or 'green capitalism' can magically change the trajectory. The extractivist/expansionist obsessions of today's high-energy/advanced-technology world have brought us to a point where a continued large-scale human presence on the planet is no longer certain; some of the most vulnerable populations around the world already face catastrophic conditions and there's no guarantee that the affluent will be protected indefinitely from similar fates. Yet critical voices are drowned out by the modern world's assertion that there is no possible challenge to 'our way of life', especially in the United States.

Facing honestly the challenges posed by racist, capitalist, imperialist, and high-energy industrial systems is difficult, but perhaps even more difficult is facing the deep pathology of

our sex/gender system. That system has a name—patriarchy—
the origins of which take us back further into human history,
not just centuries but several thousand years, to the beginning
of institutionalized male dominance, when "men discovered
how to turn 'difference' into dominance" and "laid the
ideological foundation for all systems of hierarchy, inequality,
and exploitation."[2]

Men's assertion in patriarchy of a right to control women's
sexuality and reproduction, backed by violence, was central
to a process that created a world rigidly ordered by 'power-
over'—power defined as the ability to impose your will on
others or to resist that imposition by others, contrasted
with the collaborative conception of 'power-with'.[3] This
domination/subordination dynamic would come to define
virtually all interactions, both within the human family and
between humans and the larger living world. The pathology
of patriarchy, the idea that one group of people should control
another—even own them, own even life itself—is at the core
of today's crises. Feminist resistance, by older veterans of the
women's movement and younger natives of the digital world,
continues to challenge that pathology, with some success in
some places and times. But the patriarchal sex/gender system
has proved resilient, and everywhere institutionalized male
dominance continues to structure our lives and influence our
understanding of ourselves.

2 Gerda Lerner, *Why History Matters: Life and Thought* (New York: Oxford
University Press, 1997), p. 133.

3 The distinction between 'power-over' and 'power-with' is usually credited to
Mary Parker Follett, a theorist, political organizer, and social activist who
wrote several influential books in the first half of the twentieth century. The
terms are used today in a variety of academic, political, and business settings.
I first encountered this term in discussions with feminist activists. See Amy
Allen, "Feminist Perspectives on Power," in Edward N. Zalta, ed., *The Stanford
Encyclopedia of Philosophy* (Summer 2014). <http://plato.stanford.edu/archives/
sum2014/entries/feminist-power/>

These are difficult realities to face, and so it is hardly surprising that the world is full of denial and diversions, by people on the top and on the bottom and everywhere in between. We are, and should be, afraid. Let me make it more personal: I am terrified of what humans have created and of our trajectory. I am terrified not only of the unjust and unsustainable systems that we humans have created, but of the willingness of so many to deny reality or divert attention from it. This book is part of my ongoing struggle to deal with that terror. I take seriously James Baldwin's advice about dealing with terror: "If you've got any sense, you realize you'd better not run. Ain't no place to run. So, you walk toward it. At least that way you'll know what hit you."[4]

If we want to understand what has hit us and what is likely to keep hitting us in the future, probably with increasing force, we need to get radical. Although the term 'radical' is often used to dismiss people or ideas as 'crazy' or 'extreme', in this context it describes an analysis that seeks to understand, address, and eventually eliminate the root causes of social injustice and ecological unsustainability. To make sense of these crises, I believe we need feminist analysis, an intellectual project to understand the illegitimate structures of authority under which we live. We need feminism, a political movement to organize resistance to that authority. We need feminists, people who are willing to walk toward what is hitting us. Feminist analysis informing feminist movements that strengthen the resolve of feminists will not alone save us—lots of other radical perspectives and movements are necessary—but without a

---

4   James Baldwin, interviewed by Mavis Nicholson, "Mavis on Four" (1987). <https://www.youtube.com/watch?v=3Wht4NSf7E4> Baldwin, an accomplished U.S. novelist, and essayist from the 1950s until his death in 1987, was a leading voice for civil rights and social justice across the board.

radical feminism contributing to resistance, there is no hope of saving ourselves.

The historian Gerda Lerner, whose work has helped us understand the origins of patriarchy, expressed this hope in the feminist project when she wrote:

> The system of patriarchy is a historic construct; it has a beginning; it will have an end. Its time seems to have nearly run its course—it no longer serves the needs of men or women and in its inextricable linkage to militarism, hierarchy, and racism it threatens the very existence of life on earth.[5]

My deepest fear is that Lerner is wrong about our ability to transcend patriarchy, that no matter how obvious it becomes that the systems we humans have devised are destructive—to the point of threatening to take us over the cliff—we won't turn back. My deepest fear is not only that the people in power won't turn back, but that it may be impossible to find a way to turn back at this point, that we are too close to the cliff with too much momentum. Lerner is right that patriarchy doesn't serve the needs of human beings, male or female, but it does continue to serve some people's perceived need for wealth and status, and those perceptions create powerful motivations to deny and divert.

Sadly, in the past two decades a radical feminist critique of patriarchy not only has lost ground in the United States but has been rejected in some feminist circles. While no intellectual or political movement ever could, or should, be of a single mind about how to understand the world, the disagreement within feminism about the nature of patriarchy—even about whether patriarchy is a useful concept for analyzing contemporary

---

5   Gerda Lerner, *The Creation of Patriarchy* (New York: Oxford University Press, 1986), pp. 228–229.

society—is a stark reminder of how deeply woven patriarchy is into the fabric of society and everyday life.

Despite these fears, I am committed to the ongoing effort to understand this patriarchal world and imagine a different one. This book is my attempt to contribute to the conversation about patriarchy, which means walking toward disagreements about how to understand the world and how to change it, including intensely contentious disagreements that have left feminism and feminists bitterly divided, which leads to a perfectly reasonable question: Who cares what I have to say?

Identity Politics and My Identity

I am male (with a critique)[6] and white (also with a critique),[7] born in 1958, married to a woman (though my sexual history is complicated),[8] a secular Christian (loosely defined, with a theology that rejects supernatural claims about a God or resurrected savior and sees all religious traditions as myth, symbol, poetry),[9] a lifelong citizen of the United States (another critique),[10] with two graduate degrees and a stable university faculty job that puts me in the top 20% of U.S. taxpayers. I have

---

6   Robert Jensen, *Getting Off: Pornography and the End of Masculinity* (Boston: South End Press, 2007). (Out of print, available at <http://robertwjensen. org/>.)

7   Robert Jensen, *The Heart of Whiteness: Confronting Race, Racism and White Privilege* (San Francisco: City Lights, 2005).

8   Robert Jensen, *Plain Radical: Living, Loving, and Learning to Leave the Planet Gracefully* (Berkeley, CA: Counterpoint/Soft Skull, 2015).

9   Robert Jensen, *All My Bones Shake: Seeking a Progressive Path to the Prophetic Voice* (New York: Soft Skull Press, 2009).

10   Robert Jensen, *Citizens of the Empire: The Struggle to Claim Our Humanity* (San Francisco: City Lights, 2004).

worked my entire adult life as a journalist[11] or professor,[12] jobs in which I have received considerable training and support for my writing and speaking. I'm slightly taller than the average adult male in the United States with no chronic illnesses and no noteworthy disease risk factors.

In other words, I was born in the most affluent and powerful nation-state in the history of the world, at a time of rapid economic expansion, into identity categories that came with unearned power and status, along with a fair amount of luck in the roll of the genetic dice. The only two obvious advantages I missed out on were being born wealthy and handsome.

From this social location of considerable privilege, including the key privilege of being male, I am writing a book in which I not only offer an analysis of the pathology of patriarchy but also take sides in contentious debates within feminism. At first glance, this may seem like the ultimate case of 'mansplaining', the term coined to describe the way in which men often explain things to women, typically in condescending fashion, which is especially infuriating when men try to explain gender politics to women.

So, am I extraordinarily arrogant or incredibly ignorant? Or both?

It's tempting to craft a justification for myself up front, to try to deflect the potential criticism that I have no right to weigh in on these subjects, no matter what the quality of my analysis. There are two main routes I could take to do that. First, I could point out that during my work in feminist projects over the past three decades, I have often been encouraged by women to write. That's true enough, but some women in other feminist

---

11   Robert Jensen, *Writing Dissent: Taking Radical Ideas from the Margins to the Mainstream* (New York: Peter Lang, 2001).

12   Robert Jensen, *Arguing for Our Lives: A User's Guide to Constructive Dialog* (San Francisco: City Lights, 2013).

projects have told me that I'm wrong about almost everything and have suggested that I shut up. Which women represent 'women' and can authorize me to speak?

I also could point out that some men are more likely to read feminist books written by men than those written by women, an unfortunate but accurate observation. But while I wrote this book with male readers in mind and I hope men will read this book, I also believe I offer insights of value for women. And, no matter what the sex/gender of the reader, the contentious nature of the subject guarantees some people will condemn my writing as counterproductive.

The justification for this book cannot hang on the endorsement of feminist comrades or the claim that it's only strategic outreach to men. I'm writing because I think I have something useful to say, based on decades of teaching, research, organizing, and critical self-reflection. I am not explaining women's experiences to them but using the work of feminist women to make sense of my experience of the sex/gender system in which I live in the contemporary United States. Feminist critiques of patriarchy emerged from women's struggle and are key to women's liberation, but a critique of patriarchy is also part of a larger struggle for a just and sustainable world for everyone.

To be clear: I am not arguing that identity is irrelevant to how we come to see the world, but rather that identity doesn't alone determine the value of a person's analysis of how to understand the world. From my first interaction with intellectual and political movements that examine the consequences of identity, such as feminism and critical race theory, I became aware that my failure to critically self-reflect about these subjects had left me arrogant and ignorant. Even with the considerable efforts I have made to understand these issues since then, I remain aware of how my unearned privileges not only make my daily life easier but can make it more difficult for me to see how easy I have it.

But what value are the efforts of those of us with privilege to understand the systems and structures of power that give us that privilege if we don't contribute to the struggle for a better society? Why would my goal be to educate myself about the ways that groups of which I am a member unjustly dominate others, and then remain silent? How does that advance the struggle? People in subordinated groups, when faced with repetitive questions from members of the dominant group, suggest that it's not their responsibility to always be educating us, and it's easy to understand that fatigue. Taking responsibility for my role in that process of education requires me to discuss publicly the results of the process.

Just as true, however, is that every time someone like me wants to speak is no guarantee that what I have to say contributes to the struggle. So, to sharpen the question, I'll state it personally: When should Bob speak? Like everything else in human affairs, there's no formula that provides a simple answer. Obviously, I think I should speak at this moment in history about these subjects, or I would not be writing. Some of the people I trust to hold me accountable have agreed. Just as obvious, other people will disagree (and have disagreed, in response to early versions of some of these arguments that have appeared in essays online). Some of the people who disagree will do so vehemently. The most productive disagreements are civil, but I can learn, and have learned, from uncivil criticism as well.

But I can't escape this claim, arrogant as it may sound: I'm writing because I think I have something to contribute, and I believe that I have a responsibility to contribute. And at the same time I'm writing for myself, to connect with other like-minded people, one of the ways I deal with my own fears.

My subject is the world I live in—the United States at the end of the twentieth and start of the twenty-first century. I try to situate that world in historical and global contexts, but my effort here is focused on that place and time. My goal is not to explain how the whole world works; instead, I struggle to understand my life, my place in the world.

The End of Patriarchy offers a blunt analysis of the state of the world in which we live, in plain language that is accessible to the widest possible readership. This book will be valuable if, at the end, readers have a better understanding of how they want to move forward in that world. If this book helps readers, even those who may disagree with all or part of my analysis, to gain a bit more clarity about their own views, I will consider it successful. If I manage to do that with intellectual honesty and humility, I will be satisfied.

SEX AND GENDER

As much as any political discussion and debate, inquiries into patriarchy require considerable attention to definitions of terms and explication of concepts—the sociological and scientific, the cultural and biological. Some disagreements may result from using terms in different ways, or not coming to agreement about competing definitions of a term before proceeding. So, I begin with basics.

The most basic: Human beings are organisms living in ecosystems, part of a larger living world we call the ecosphere, our home planet. Although human cognitive and linguistic capacities are—to the best of our knowledge—far more advanced than those of any other species, those capacities do not allow us to transcend the biophysical limits of the ecosphere. While there is much debate (and no plausible resolution anytime soon) about the existence of a non-material soul or mind, we should be able to agree that we are material beings and that our everyday activities are proscribed by those limits. We can use our creative capacities to imagine many alternative realities, but we live in the material reality of this world.

I take one corollary of this acceptance of our place in the ecosphere to be that there exists something we could call 'human nature', just as there is pigeon nature or barley nature or algae nature. That simply means that every organism has a genetic endowment that makes some things possible and some things impossible—there are parameters within which any organism, including the human, operates. Everyday experience demonstrates that human nature is widely variable, that any two humans who seem pretty much the same can act in dramatically different ways in the same situation, and that there's little we can predict with certainty about any specific human's behavior in a particular situation.

Take the example of whether violence is a part of human nature. There is no reason to believe that any human society has been 100% free of aggressive physical acts by one person against another. We are a species capable of violence, and it's likely that all humans—even those who may never have been violent in their lives, if such a human has ever existed—have the capacity for violence. The real questions are, under what social conditions is violence more or less likely, and what individual differences, interacting with those social conditions, might increase or decrease the likelihood of violent action? We never know as much as we would like to know about these kinds of questions and are usually left to act on informed hunches based on limited evidence.

For example, military organizations have learned that even when killing is socially supported in war, it is part of many individuals' human nature to avoid killing other people, which is counterproductive in battle situations where the military's goal is to eliminate opposing soldiers. Military officials have learned that training can be designed not only to teach soldiers to use killing tools effectively but also to reduce the psychological/spiritual impediments to taking another life, and the implementation of that kind of training has been successful.[13] This does not mean every human being can be trained to kill on command[14]—there is considerable individual variation within the human species—but socialization shapes the expression of that variation, and there are patterns in how people respond to that socialization.

This perception of patterns is the best we can hope for when trying to understand ourselves, our behavior, and the social norms that shape that behavior. We look to the parameters set by biology and do our best to discern the patterns within those parameters. Since anything that human beings do is, by definition, within our nature to do, the question "what is human nature?" should be replaced with questions about which aspects of our nature tend to dominate under various conditions.

Another example involving violence: Is it human nature to beat a child? At first glance, that seems like an awful question—we should love and nurture children, and decent people don't beat children. But children are beaten regularly enough that the capacity clearly is part of human nature. The important questions are, once again: Under what conditions is such violence more likely to occur, and what differences between individuals might influence the likelihood of the violence? Anyone who says, "I would never beat a child" might consider how one's rejection of such violence under ordinary conditions could change in extreme situations that produce inordinate stress.

---

13   Dave Grossman, *On Killing: The Psychological Cost of Learning to Kill in War and Society* (New York: Back Bay Books, 2009, revised edition).

14   For an extensive analysis, see Kathleen Barry, *Unmaking War Remaking Men: How Empathy Can Reshape Our Politics, Our Soldiers and Ourselves* (Santa Rosa, CA: Phoenix Rising Press, 2010; North Melbourne, Australia: Spinifex Press, 2010).

This helps us navigate the meaning of 'essentialism', a term commonly used in discussions of sex/gender. In certain circles, the assertion that one has an essentialist position on sex/gender is a pejorative. Accusations of essentialism arise often in discussions about a question such as, "Are female humans by nature—that is, essentially—better at making emotional connections, especially with children, than male humans?" A strongly essentialist claim (all female humans are always more adept at emotional engagement than all male humans) is silly, easily refuted by experience. But is a strongly anti-essentialist claim (there are absolutely no differences in levels or styles of emotional connection between female and male humans) any less silly? A reasonable proposal is that the type and intensity of emotional connections are largely a product of how females and males are socialized, and that there will be considerable variation—between societies that have different ways of socializing females and males, and within a society between individuals, affected greatly by early experience. But that proposal is, in a sense, simply an admission that we don't know much about the answer.

The question we want to answer is more vexing: Even acknowledging that socialization will have considerable influence, is there something about the biological differences between female and male humans that make females more likely on average to be better at making emotional connections than males? Is the fact that males do not give birth to children relevant to the discussion? Given the centrality of reproduction to all organisms, and the long period of care that human infants require, this material difference between male and female humans certainly could be relevant, but just as certainly there is no simple or obvious answer. To make a strongly essentialist claim seems unwarranted, as does making a strongly anti-essentialist claim. We lack reliable evidence for either of those positions.

The answer is potentially important, and not merely to satisfy intellectual curiosity. Imagine that by some research method currently far beyond the capacity of existing science, we could determine that females are 'naturally' 18% better at emotional connections than males, and that extra efforts to teach males to be more emotionally connected can only slightly reduce that difference. If we knew that to be accurate, should we shape social arrangements to put females in roles that require more emotional intelligence and put males into other roles? Is the benefit to society in achieving the maximal level of collective emotional connection most important? Or does society benefit when males' abilities are improved, even if only slightly? Or perhaps all this concern about emotional connection makes people insufficiently tough-minded and is detrimental to developing economic efficiency, and therefore males should be in charge of emotional matters so that there's less fussing about it.

My point is simple: Arguments about public policy that are based on simplistic, speculative claims about human nature should be met with considerable skepticism. Whatever one's view, it's difficult to imagine answering the question by asserting a strong essentialist claim that we need not consider anything beyond our genetic endowments as male and female. It seems equally difficult to imagine defending the claim that the physical differences between male and female could not possibly have any bearing on the question. If we jam this into the common 'nature versus nurture' framework, we might conclude—as we almost always do—that there is a complex interplay between genetic endowment and epigenetic factors, which set the parameters for human behavior, and socialization, which not only shapes individuals' behavior but affects the material reality under which the process goes forward.

Definitions of Sex and Gender

These observations are background to the important distinction between sex and gender, the biological and the cultural, what one historian describes as "the single most important feminist theoretical contribution to social theory … the social structures and meanings attributed to sex difference."[15] Examining that distinction helps identify points of agreement and disagreement, both in the larger society and within feminism.

Borrowing from historian Joan Scott, gender is "the social organization of sexual difference."[16] This sex/gender framework emerged in the 1970s, with perhaps the first clear articulation in sociologist Ann Oakley's 1972 book:

> 'Sex' is a word that refers to the biological differences between male and female: the visible difference in genitalia, the related difference in procreative function. 'Gender' however is a matter of culture: it refers to the social classification into 'masculine' and 'feminine'.[17]

---

15 Linda Gordon, "The Women's Liberation Moment," in Dorothy Sue Cobble, Linda Gordon, and Astrid Henry, *Feminism Unfinished: A Short, Surprising History of American Women's Movements* (New York: Liveright/W.W. Norton and Co., 2014), p. 85.

16 Joan Wallach Scott, *Gender and the Politics of History* (New York: Columbia University Press, 1988), p. 2.

17 Ann Oakley, *Sex, Gender and Society*, (Farnham, UK: Ashgate, 1985, revised edition), pp. 21–22.

Let's start with the biology. There are three categories of biological human sex: male, female, and intersex.[18] The vast majority of humans are born with male or female reproductive systems, secondary sexual characteristics, and a chromosomal structure that includes two sex chromosomes that are either XX (female) or XY (male). There are some people (the size of this category would depend on what degree of ambiguity is used to mark it; the common figure is 1 in 2000[19]) born with a reproductive or sexual anatomy that doesn't fit the definitions of female or male—anomalies in sex chromosomes, gonads, and/or anatomical sex. One researcher reports that using the expansive definition "intersexual in some form," 1.7% of people are born intersex,[20] and the estimate for those receiving some kind of 'corrective' genital surgery is between 0.1 and 0.2%.[21] The existence of people born intersex does not negate the sexually dimorphic character of the species. As philosopher Rebecca Reilly-Cooper has pointed out, the fact that there are humans born without two functional legs or with problems

---

18   "'Intersex' is a general term used for a variety of conditions in which a person is born with a reproductive or sexual anatomy that doesn't seem to fit the typical definitions of female or male. For example, a person might be born appearing to be female on the outside, but having mostly male-typical anatomy on the inside. Or a person may be born with genitals that seem to be in-between the usual male and female types—for example, a girl may be born with a noticeably large clitoris, or lacking a vaginal opening, or a boy may be born with a notably small penis, or with a scrotum that is divided so that it has formed more like labia. Or a person may be born with mosaic genetics, so that some of her cells have XX chromosomes and some of them have XY." "What is intersex?" Intersex Society of North America. <http://www.isna.org/faq/what_is_intersex>

19   "How common is intersex?" Intersex Society of North America. <http://www.isna.org/faq/frequency>

20   Anne Fausto-Sterling, "The Five Sexes, Revisited," *Sciences*, 40:3 (July/August 2000): 20.

21   Melanie Blackless, et al., "How Sexually Dimorphic Are We? Review and Synthesis," *American Journal of Human Biology*, 12:2 (March/April 2000): 151–166.

that preclude them from walking upright does not mean that humans are not bipedal.[22]

These categories are biological—based on the material reality of who can potentially reproduce with whom. They are called 'sex'. Beyond the category of 'sex' (the biological differences between males and females), there is 'gender' (the non-biological meaning societies create out of sex differences). Gender plays out in a variety of ways, including gender roles (assigning males and females to different social, political, or economic roles); gender norms (expecting males and females to comply with different norms of behavior and appearance); gendered traits and virtues (assuming that males and females will be intellectually, emotionally, or morally different from each other); and gender symbolism (using gender in the description of animals, inanimate objects, or ideas).[23]

In contemporary society, we routinely talk about sex in terms of 'males' and 'females' (a biological distinction that exists independent of any particular culture's understanding), and gender in terms of 'masculinity' and 'femininity' (cultural distinctions that depend on how humans in a particular society understand the meaning of the biological distinction). The terms 'men' and 'women', or 'boys' and 'girls', are used by different people in different contexts to mean either sex or gender, which can be a source of confusion in political debate. (I use male/female when referring to sex differences rooted in biology and man/woman or boy/girl when referring to gender roles rooted in cultural constructions of masculinity/femininity.) For someone in the sex category intersex, we

---

22   Rebecca Reilly-Cooper, "Sex and Gender: A Beginner's Guide" (2015). <http://sexandgenderintro.com/>

23   Elizabeth Anderson, "Feminist Epistemology and Philosophy of Science," in Edward N. Zalta, ed., *The Stanford Encyclopedia of Philosophy* (Fall 2012). <http://plato.stanford.edu/archives/fall2012/entries/feminism-epistemology>

have no commonly used terminology, and traditionally this culture has attempted to force such people into male or female categories, often with negative consequences.[24]

The claim of some theorists such as Judith Butler that not only gender but sex itself is a social construction is difficult to understand. Since we organize our world through language, any human naming of the world is, in some sense, a social construction—understanding is shared socially through language. But that's a trivial use of the term, and the question is, to what degree is an assertion about the material world rooted in a reality that we can trust as being accurate independent of human perception and practices? I confess that I find postmodern claims that we should understand "the construal of 'sex' no longer as a bodily given on which the construct of gender is artificially imposed, but as a cultural norm which governs the materialization of bodies"[25] to be unhelpful.

If a concept is a 'social construction', that means it can be deconstructed, and we could live without it. As Marilyn Frye puts it:

> To deconstruct a concept is to analyze it in a way which reveals its construction—both in the temporal sense of its birth and development over time and in a certain cultural and political matrix, and in the sense of its own present structure, its meaning, and its relation to other concepts. One of the most impressive aspects of such an analysis is the revelation of the 'contingency' of the concept, i.e. the fact that it is only the accidental collaboration of various historical events and circumstances that brought that

---

24 Katrina Karkazis, *Fixing Sex: Intersex, Medical Authority, and Lived Experience* (Durham, NC: Duke University Press, 2008); and Elizabeth Weil, "What if It's (Sort of) a Boy and (Sort of) a Girl?" *New York Times Magazine*, September 24, 2006. <http://www.nytimes.com/2006/09/24/magazine/24intersexkids. html?fta=y&_r=0>

25 Judith Butler, *Bodies that Matter: On the Discursive Limits of 'Sex'* (New York: Routledge, 1993), pp. 2–3.

concept into being, and the fact that *there could be a world of sense without that concept in it* (emphasis added).[26]

In Frye's terms, there cannot be a world of sense without an understanding of male and female. No matter what understanding any human society has of sex differences, human reproduction doesn't take place without a male and a female human (even high-tech medical interventions start with sperm and egg, male and female). I don't understand how the claim that sexed bodies are 'discursively constructed' could possibly change that, and so the claim that the sex categories of male and female are a social construction remains incoherent to me. When a colleague challenged my position, she suggested that the science of biology is just one story about sex differences. If that's true, I said, is there a story that anyone could tell, scientific or otherwise, in which I, as a male human, could carry, give birth to, and breastfeed a child?

Sex/Gender and Race

A comparison to racial categories helps make this point. Unlike sex categories, racial categories are biologically arbitrary, a social construction in the deep sense. Racial categories are attached to observable physical differences (such as skin color and hair texture), and there are some characteristics (such as reactions to a specific drug or susceptibility to a specific disease) in which there are some patterns based on ancestors' region-of-origin. But unlike sex categories, the division of people into racial categories is not tied to any biological difference or characteristic that is important to human survival.

---

26 Marilyn Frye, *Willful Virgin: Essays in Feminism 1976–1992* (Freedom, CA: Crossing Press, 1992), p. 163.

Borrowing from Frye, there could be a world of sense without the concept of 'race' in it. We could easily imagine living in human societies with no concept of racial distinctions; observable physical differences would remain, but skin color would be no more relevant for creating categories than the size of one's ears, for example. People have different sized ears, and we could arbitrarily divide the world into the large-eared versus small-eared, but we don't. The genetic differences between humans that are rooted in ancestors' region-of-origin are extremely small and are not the basis for a meaningful biological concept of race. Race, then, is a deeply social construct, using real physical differences to categorize, but differences that have meaning only because of a social process. The modern idea of race, emerging from Europe during its era of conquest and colonization, is the result of history.

But, to restate the obvious, sex categories are different. Human reproduction depends on the physical difference between males and females. This is not an argument that sexuality has no function other than reproduction, which often leads to heterosexist assumptions and anti-lesbian/gay politics, but rather a simple observation about material realities. For humans to mark reproductive differences—to see male and female as distinctively different—is inevitable; the process is not arbitrary.

We can imagine a world with no race categories, but it would be impossible—outside of science fiction—to construct a world without sex categories. Our eventual goal, then, should be to eliminate the concept of race, though in the short term we must retain the categories to deal honestly with the pernicious effects of the social/political realities of white supremacy and racism.

Biologically determined sex categories are here to stay, but can we reject the idea of socially constructed gender categories? After all, if gender is socially constructed, with variations in that construction across time and place, then we should be able to choose not to construct gender at all, right? Is eliminating any conception of gender (beyond the ever-present awareness of which category of human bears children) from our lives possible? I think not, for two simple reasons: (1) Reproduction is central to organisms, and sex differences (male and female) are central to human reproduction; and (2) we human beings constantly use our cognitive capacities to understand the world, even when we don't have a clear way to understand most of what happens, and then we talk about it. Whatever our cognitive limits, we are meaning-seeking and story-telling organisms; we want to understand whatever is in us and around us. When we don't have a definitive account of a phenomenon (which is most of the time, about most things), we still tell stories about what it means (that is, we make stuff up).

Put those things together—the centrality of sex differences to our continued existence, and our meaning-seeking/story-telling tendencies—and it's difficult to imagine any human community not telling stories about what sex differences mean beyond the obvious biology of reproduction. That suggests we will always be telling some kind of stories about gender. Can anyone imagine a human community that takes no notice of the physical differences between females and males, except when males and females have intercourse to conceive and when females are giving birth and breastfeeding? Can anyone imagine people ever not being inquisitive about the deeper meaning of such a basic difference—not creating art that explores the meaning of sex differences beyond reproduction, not constructing symbols that mark sex differences?

In short: By 'gender', I mean human stories about what sex differences mean beyond reproduction, and the social organization that follows from them. If a society were to tell stories asserting that there are no distinctions between male and female humans beyond reproduction, that is still a gender system, one that emphasizes the similarities between male and female rather than potential differences.

Some feminists have suggested that we must try to imagine abolishing gender, including feminists on whose work I rely, and/or who are personal friends. But on this point I disagree with them: Since some sort of gender system—meaning assigned to sex differences that go beyond merely taking note of reproduction—is inevitable, we should work with gender rather than imagine transcending it. The fact that gender-in-patriarchy is a system used by men to oppress women does not mean we cannot construct gender-for-liberation, stories about sex differences that promote collaboration and egalitarianism rather than hierarchy and domination. Humans can create, and in the past have created, stories and symbols about sex differences that did just that; pre-patriarchal human societies demonstrate that gender-role differentiation can be compatible with egalitarian values.[27]

We can, and should, make judgments about the stories people tell about gender; some claims about the meaning of gender can be an impediment to human flourishing. In patriarchy, gendered norms and practices are often brutal and destructive, but there could be non-patriarchal claims about the meaning of gender that foster that flourishing. I certainly understand the argument that accepting the inevitability of gender means that gender roles/norms will inevitably limit humans' ability to flourish—the fear that retaining the idea that male and female are different enough to require gender

---

27 For examples, see Judy Foster with Marlene Derlet, *Invisible Women of Prehistory: Three Million Years of Peace, Six Thousand Years of War* (North Melbourne, Australia: Spinifex Press, 2013).

stories means bad things are unavoidable. I do not believe those bad things are inevitable. But in the end, whether or not we like the idea of gender—the meaning humans make of sex differences—the reality of sex differences means we will live with some kind of gender stories, and our task is to strive for gender roles and norms that foster rather than impede stable, decent human communities.

Caution about Gender Claims

Human stories about gender may be inevitable, but we should be extremely careful about the kinds of claims we make in those stories, which means being aware of the limits of our knowledge about our own psychology. Male and female humans are defined by different roles in reproduction, but claims about additional sexed traits or virtues—any potential intellectual, emotional, and moral differences between males and females that may be connected to biological sex—should be carefully scrutinized.

I approach this from a cautious position in intellectual terms, not only acknowledging our extremely limited knowledge about human psychology that we have at the moment but also recognizing that we do not have the intellectual ability to allow us to say much of anything in the near future. At our current level of understanding, with the research tools we have available to us, it's unlikely we'll know much more anytime soon about these questions concerning potential intellectual/emotional/moral differences based on sex. In other words, this is one of the many questions about a complex world in which we are fundamentally ignorant—what we don't know overwhelms what we do know. The latest discoveries from neuroscience, as impressive as they may be, add only a few more drops to the bucket of human knowledge that is a long way from filled.

We know that males and females are more alike in biological terms than different. We don't know much about the effect of those differences in terms of intellectual/emotional/moral processes, nor do we know much about how malleable any differences that do exist might be. The existence of patriarchy indicates that some differences are there—men's subordination of women wouldn't have arisen without some biological differences that made a difference beyond reproduction and led to men institutionalizing that dominance behavior rather than women. But that fact says nothing about our ability to construct a society that transcends patriarchy; it's certainly plausible that we have the capacity to overcome whatever biological differences led to patriarchal societies.

Simply put, once again: While there's no doubt that a large part of our behavior is rooted in our DNA, there's also no doubt that how our genetic endowment plays out in the world is highly influenced by culture. Beyond that, it's difficult to say much with any certainty. It's true that only female humans can bear children. Not all females do that, of course, but only females can. That fact likely has some bearing on patterns in some aspects of men's and women's personalities. But we don't know much about what the effect is, and it's not likely we ever will know much.

Our culture's obsession with gender differences produces a recurring intellectual fad (called 'evolutionary psychology' this time around, and 'sociobiology' in a previous incarnation) that wants to explain all complex behaviors as simple evolutionary adaptations—if a pattern of human behavior exists, it must be because it's adaptive in some ways. In the long run, that's true. But in the short-term—the arena in which we have to analyze and make choices—it is hardly a convincing argument to say,

"Look at how men and women behave differently; it must be because men and women are incredibly, fundamentally different" when a system of power (patriarchy) has been imposing social differences between men and women through coercion and violence for a few thousand years. It may be that in the long run, patriarchy has not been a successful adaptation and will lead to the extinction of the species. As we look around the world at the threats to the ecosphere from unsustainable human systems deeply rooted in patriarchy's domination/subordination dynamic, that's not only plausible but increasingly likely. That suggests that patriarchy is an evolutionary dead-end.

Human nature made patriarchy possible, but that does not mean patriarchy is immutable.[28] Making sensible decisions about our sex/gender system must start with a reckoning of the history and contemporary practices in patriarchy, recognizing that *gender in patriarchy* is a category that *established and reinforces inequality.*

---

28   Barbara Smuts, "The Evolutionary Origins of Patriarchy," *Human Nature*, 6:1 (1995): 1–32.

PATRIARCHY
AND FEMINISM

1. Patriarchy is the appropriate term to describe the majority of human societies for the past several thousand years, including contemporary U.S. society.
2. Radical feminism is the most coherent critique of patriarchy and should be at the heart of the comprehensive radical analyses needed to challenge the domination/subordination dynamic that defines the contemporary world.

When I first encountered those two claims, nearly thirty years ago as I began graduate school, I resisted. As a man socialized in patriarchy, both those claims seemed extreme, and extremely dangerous to my well-being. But within months of starting serious study of the sex/gender system, I realized that radical feminism not only helped me understand the world in which I lived but helped me understand myself.

As I continued studying, I learned that both of those claims not only were contentious in the general culture—it's hardly surprising that a patriarchal culture would reject a critique of patriarchy—but also within feminism. I was told that this radical perspective, which was so intellectually and politically productive for me, was suspect because it was a 'totalizing' theory imposing a 'grand narrative' that could not be taken seriously by sophisticated thinkers. As a new graduate student, I desperately wanted to be a sophisticated thinker, but I couldn't shake the idea that the radical feminist analyses I was reading were compelling.

To be clear: I'm against totalizing, if by that we mean presenting an account of human society that pretends to identify every relevant variable and explain every outcome. We work to perceive patterns in human affairs, but identifying patterns gives us at best a rough approximation of events and their causes and does not offer the potential precision of scientific theories. I'm also against grand narratives, if by that we mean the arrogant and/or naïve assertion that one story can answer all questions about how people have constructed, and should construct, systems and institutions to distribute power and resources.

With those cautions, when we define and describe patriarchy, can there be stable, coherent categories of 'woman' and 'man' that we can use as the basis for analysis and political action? Marilyn Frye points out that some generalization is necessary, because we "have to have some sort of genuinely general generality to have theory, philosophy, politics," but that the generalizations which emerge from pattern perception need not be reductive or totalitarian. "Naming patterns is like charting the prevailing winds over a continent," she writes, "which does not imply that every individual and item in the landscape is identically affected."[29]

---

29 Marilyn Frye, *Willful Virgin: Essays in Feminism 1976–1992* (Freedom, CA: Crossing Press, 1992), pp. 64, 66.

I take a simple lesson from the common observation that life is complicated: Be cautious about what you claim to know for certain. But I take an equally important lesson from the reality of human suffering: We have an obligation to do our best to understand how the world works so that we can contribute to movements seeking a more just distribution of power and resources in order to promote human flourishing and a more sustainable human presence on the planet.

So, we inevitably will tell stories about the patterns we perceive. They need not be totalizing or grand, but our non-totalizing not-grand narratives need to be detailed enough to offer meaningful guidance in the struggle for justice and sustainability. In telling those stories, we sometimes will make mistakes in gathering and interpreting information. Through critical self-reflection, individually and collectively, we can modify our accounts of the patterns and adjust the policies we pursue based on those accounts so that we can achieve greater social justice and ecological sustainability. Frye embraces this possibility when she distinguishes the imposition of truth claims by 'experts' from the method of feminist consciousness-raising:

> The experiences of each woman and of the women collectively generate a new web of meaning. Our process has been one of discovering, recognizing, and creating patterns—patterns within which experience made a new kind of sense, or, in many instances, for the first time made any sense at all. Instead of bringing a phase of enquiry to closure by summing up what is known, as other ways of generalizing do, pattern recognition/ construction opens fields of meaning and generates new interpretive possibilities. Instead of drawing conclusions from observations, it generates observations.[30]

---

30 *Ibid.*, p. 65.

After three decades of attempts at such critical self-reflection, my early commitment to a radical feminist analysis of patriarchy has deepened. Three decades of paying close attention to cultural/political/economic/ecological trends in U.S. society leave me more persuaded than ever that such radical feminist analyses are the most compelling account of the sex/gender system available, and are crucial to a much-needed comprehensive radical analysis of the unjust and unsustainable systems that define the world today.

Rather than weigh in on all the theoretical debates that have surfaced in feminism in recent decades, I will sketch the framework that has helped me grapple with sex/gender issues, renewing my introductory disclaimer: In trying to understand how to organize my own life, I come to judgments about the nature of the society in which I live from a position of considerable privilege, and others may deem those judgments wrong or objectionable. But claiming that someone with privilege shouldn't speak about his intellectual positions and political conclusions because of those disagreements—in this case, a man speaking about patriarchy and feminism—would, paradoxically, let privileged people off the hook for defending their political and moral decisions. Every day all of us—men and women—make decisions on how to act in the world based on an analysis of the sex/gender system, whether or not we articulate that analysis in public or are even aware of our analysis. In my view, it's more productive to disagree openly and defend one's assumptions, definitions, evidence, and logic.

Patriarchy

'Patriarchy', from Greek meaning 'rule of the father', can be narrowly understood as the organization of a human community (from a family to a larger society) that gives a male ruler dominance over other men, and overall gives men control over women. More generally, patriarchy is used to describe various systems of institutionalized male dominance, though some historians argue that the term should not be used so generally, that patriarchy is 'father domination' based on generational authority and a specific conception of family power, which is just one form of male dominance.[31]

While patriarchal systems developed thousands of years ago, the contemporary feminist critique of patriarchy as an all-encompassing cultural/political/economic system that disadvantages/subordinates/oppresses women emerged in the second half of the twentieth century; Kate Millett is usually cited as the first feminist writer to use the term in this way, in her 1970 book *Sexual Politics*.[32] In contemporary social analysis, patriarchy is typically understood as "a system of social structures and practices in which men dominate, oppress and exploit women." In that definition from sociologist Sylvia Walby, "social structures" is a key term that "clearly implies rejection both of biological determinism, and the notion that every individual man is in a dominant position and every woman in a subordinate one."[33]

Similarly, historian Gerda Lerner defined patriarchy as "the manifestation and institutionalization of male dominance over women and children in the family and the extension of male dominance over women in the society in general." Patriarchy implies, she continued, "that men hold power in all the important institutions of society and that women are deprived of access to such power. It does not imply that women are

---

31   Linda Gordon and Allen Hunter, "Not All Male Dominance Is Patriarchal," *Radical History Review,* 71 (Spring 1998): 71–83.

32   Kate Millett, *Sexual Politics* (Garden City, NY: Doubleday, 1970).

33   Sylvia Walby, *Theorizing Patriarchy* (Oxford, UK: Basil Blackwell, 1990), p. 20.

either totally powerless or totally deprived of rights, influence and resources."[34] The specific forms that patriarchy takes differ depending on time and place, "but the essence remains: some men control property and hold power over other men and over most women; men or male-dominated institutions control the sexuality and reproduction of females; most of the powerful institutions in society are dominated by men."[35]

Psychologist Sandra Bem used the term "androcentrism" to describe this same "privileging of males, male experience, and the male perspective" that leads to men defining women as the other, with a focus on

> (1) her difference from, and her inferiority to, the universal standard or norm that he sees himself as naturally representing; (2) her domestic and reproductive function within the family or household that he sees himself as naturally heading; and (3) her ability to stimulate and to satisfy his own sexual appetite, which he finds both exciting and threatening.[36]

These definitions don't contend that all women have the same experience in patriarchy, or that 'feminine' has been defined in the same way everywhere for all time. But, as historian Judith Bennett puts it, 'woman' "usually acts as a stable category—for its time and place—that can critically determine a person's life chances."[37] That pattern of women's relative disadvantage vis-à-vis men is clear, according to Bennett: "Almost every girl born

---

34 Gerda Lerner, *The Creation of Patriarchy* (New York: Oxford University Press, 1986), p. 239.

35 Gerda Lerner, *Why History Matters: Life and Thought* (New York: Oxford University Press, 1997), p. 147.

36 Sandra Lipsitz Bem, *The Lenses of Gender: Transforming the Debate on Sexual Inequality* (New Haven, CT: Yale University Press, 1993), p. 46.

37 Judith M. Bennett, *History Matters: Patriarchy and the Challenge of Feminism* (Philadelphia: University of Pennsylvania Press, 2006), p. 9.

today will face more constraints and restrictions than will be encountered by a boy who is born today into *the same social circumstances as that girl*."[38]

Where and when did this idea of hierarchical organization and male dominance take root in human societies? Patriarchy, along with other entrenched forms of hierarchy, is a relatively recent development in *Homo sapiens'* 200,000 years on the planet, an observation that challenges the conventional 'caveman' story about the history of sex/gender and power. The cartoon image of a prehistoric man clubbing a woman and then dragging her by her hair, presumably going off to mate with/rape her, sums up a common view: Because males are, on average, physically larger than females, males must have dominated since the beginning of the human species. While there are always debates over history, and even more frequent debates over pre-history (the period of human existence before written records), there is no evidence for this common view of patriarchy-since-the-beginning.

The consensus in anthropology is that the small band-level hunting/gathering societies, which were the norm for most of human history, were generally egalitarian, with no institutionalized dominance of male over female, or vice versa. In most hunter/gatherer bands, males did most or all of the big-game hunting, and females gathered plant foods and sometimes hunted smaller game. The caveman view assumes that male big-game hunting gave men greater value and status, but the majority of calories in these societies came from the females' gathering—women were the key providers as well as primary caregivers for small children. Social systems around the world varied, but most were neither hierarchical nor male-dominated.

---

38 *Ibid.*, p. 10.

Judy Foster and Marlene Derlet, as the subtitle of their book indicates, analyze the rise of patriarchy in the past six-thousand years, working with the 'Kurgan hypothesis' of the late archaeologist Maria Gimbutas, which focuses on the development of patriarchy among people speaking a Proto Indo-European language coming from the steppes of eastern Europe after domesticating horses. Foster and Derlet explain that pre-patriarchal societies were often matriarchal, but not in the sense of women dominating men. Instead, 'matriarchy' (or what Gimbutas called 'matristic' societies[39] and Marilyn French called 'matricentry', "small simple societies centered about mothers"[40]) should be understood as describing more egalitarian societies that typically were matrilineal but with few restrictions on men or women based on sex differences.[41]

Lerner analyzed the emergence of patriarchy in the ancient Near East around 3000 BCE, showing how the subordination of women and male control of their reproductive role preceded the development of private property and served as a model for the subsequent subordination of other humans by dominant ruling classes:

> Economic oppression and exploitation are based as much on the commodification of female sexuality and the appropriation by men of women's labor power and her reproductive power as on the direct economic acquisition of resources and persons.[42]

---

39   Marija Gimbutas, *The Civilization of the Goddess: The World of Old Europe* (San Francisco: Harper, 1991).

40   Marilyn French, *From Eve to Dawn: A History of Women, Volume 1: Origins* (Toronto: McArthur & Co., 2002), p. 39.

41   Judy Foster with Marlene Derlet, *Invisible Women of Prehistory: Three Million Years of Peace, Six Thousand Years of War* (North Melbourne, Australia: Spinifex Press, 2013), pp. 18–19.

42   Lerner, *The Creation of Patriarchy*, p. 216.

The development of patriarchy is in part a product of the agricultural revolution, the domestication of plants and animals that humans began about 10,000 years ago. In agricultural societies, the communal and cooperative ethic of those hunter/gatherers was eventually replaced with ideas of private ownership and patrimony that led to men controlling women's reproduction and claiming ownership of women. Here's a short account, summarizing Lerner:

In the Neolithic Era, as larger and more hierarchal societies were developing, females increasingly became seen as a commodity in what anthropologists have called 'the exchange of women'—groups giving women to another group for marriage alliances, as gestures of hospitality, or as part of rituals aimed at ensuring abundance. Lerner argues this system was not the result of a conspiracy of evil males, but instead was created by men and women because the practices were initially beneficial for all. Whatever the original motivations, Lerner points out the destructive consequences:

> The sexuality of women, consisting of their sexual and their reproductive capacities and services, was commodified, even prior to the creation of archaic states [in the second millennium BCE]. The development of agriculture in the Neolithic age fostered the inter-tribal 'exchange of women', not only as a means of avoiding incessant warfare by the cementing of marriage alliances, but also because societies with more women could produce more children. In contrast to the needs of hunting/ gathering societies, agriculturalists could use the labor of children to increase production and accumulate surpluses. The first gender-defined social role for women was to be those who were exchanged in marriage transactions. For men, the obverse gender role was to be those who do the exchanging or define the terms of the exchanges. As a result of such widespread practices, men had rights in women which women did not have in men.

Women themselves became a resource, acquired by men, much as the land was acquired by men.[43]

With the rise of agriculture, women's labor—not only their productive labor in the fields and villages but also their reproductive labor to produce the children needed for the increasing amount of work in the fields—became a resource that patriarchs claimed to own. And, as larger-scale warfare became more common, especially during periods of economic scarcity, females were captured and enslaved. This, Lerner argues, became the template for eventually enslaving men.

In pre-patriarchal societies, male and female humans had different roles that grew out of the realities of sex differences. The sex-role differentiation that was a result of biology (females bear children and breastfeed) was the basis for gender-role differentiation (males, who didn't nurse infants, hunted and females gathered). While there was no single organizational style of hunter/gatherer society, Lerner points out that this differentiation did not automatically result in hierarchy and inequality:

The biological difference between men and women became significant as a marker of subordination only by the cultural elaboration of difference into a mark of degradation. In pre-state societies, before the full institutionalization of patriarchy men and women's biological difference found expression in a sexually based division of labor. Women, either nursing babies, pregnant or encumbered with small infants, pursued different economic activities than men did, without this difference necessarily marking them as inferior or disadvantaged. It is the cultural elaboration of 'difference' into a marker of subordination, a

---

43 Lerner, *Why History Matters*, p. 155.

social construction which is historically determined, which creates gender and structures societies into hierarchies.[44]

The agricultural revolution created a new dynamic—the ability to stockpile food created opportunities for individuals to acquire power through control of that resource, a power that was claimed by men, which raises the unavoidable question of why it was men who seized that control. Sociologist Allan Johnson suggested that the answer lies in the way "[m]en's connection to the creation of new life is invisible" and the fact that pre-patriarchal cultures lacked knowledge of how reproduction works. Men were more likely to experience themselves in ways disconnected from the larger living world and its cycles, compared with women who menstruate and bear children, making men more open to the cycle of control and fear that defines patriarchy: "Because pursuing control goes hand in hand with disconnection from the object of control, it is reasonable to suppose that as the *idea* of control emerged as a natural part of cultural evolution, men were more likely than women to see it as something to develop and exploit."[45]

It's plausible that as human populations expanded with agriculture, men were more open to control of others as a 'solution' to the problem of conflict, which would lead to greater fear of what other men might do to them, creating a spiral of control and fear. Whatever the explanation, in these patriarchal societies the generally egalitarian gender-role differentiation of hunter/gatherers went in a new direction, leading to the patriarchal reality of the contemporary world: In patriarchy, gender is a category that established and reinforces inequality.

---

44 *Ibid.*, p. 209.

45 Allan G. Johnson, *The Gender Knot: Unraveling Our Patriarchal Legacy* (Philadelphia, PA: Temple University Press, 2014, 3rd edition), p. 69.

Over thousands of years, patriarchal societies have developed various justifications for that inequality, many of which acquire the status of common sense, "that's just the way the world is." Patriarchy has proved tenacious, adjusting to challenges but blocking women from reaching full equality with men in the dominant culture. Women's status can change over time, and there are differences in status accorded to women depending on other variables. But Judith Bennett argues that these ups and downs have not transformed women as a group in relationship to men—societies operate within a "patriarchal equilibrium"[46] in which only privileged men can lay claim to that full humanity, defined as the ability to develop fully their human potential. Men with less privilege must settle for less, and some will even be accorded lower status than some women (especially those who lack race, class, or caste privilege; gender is not the only axis of inequality). But in this kind of dynamically stable system of power, women never achieve full humanity.

These analyses help us understand ourselves as individuals by illuminating the nature of the systems in which we live, though some use terms other than patriarchy. For example, sociologist Judith Lorber has argued that the term patriarchy has been overused without enough clarity but still she keeps the focus on the system: "I see gender as an institution that establishes patterns of expectations for individuals, orders the social processes of everyday life, is built into the major social organizations of society, such as the economy, ideology, the family, and politics, and is also an entity in and of itself."[47]

---

46 Judith Bennett, "History Matters: The Grand Finale," March 29, 2009. <http://girlscholar.blogspot.com/2009/03/history-matters-grand-finale-guest-post.html>; and *History Matters*, Chapter 4.

47 Judith Lorber, *Paradoxes of Gender* (New Haven, CT: Yale University Press, 1994), p. 1.

This short account of patriarchy's history reminds us that while male dominance has its roots in biological differences between male and female humans, gender inequality is a product of history and politics, not merely biology. Just as there was a pre-patriarchal period, there could be a post-patriarchal era in human affairs, a point when we transcend the hierarchy of patriarchy. It's important to remember that patriarchy is not the default setting for human societies, but rather a recent development. Restating for emphasis: In the 200,000 years of the species *Homo sapiens*, patriarchy accounts for less than 5% of our evolutionary history. If we consider the 2.5 million years of the *Homo* genus, our direct ancestors, patriarchy is less than 0.5% of our history.

We cannot predict whether the human species will create new social formations in which biological sex-role differentiation (females remain the only humans who give birth) gives rise to stories we tell about the meaning of that difference that are not based on hierarchy and that do not produce social inequality. But we can strive for such a future. The social/political movement that seeks such a future has been—and is—feminism. If humans inevitably will tell stories about the meaning they make of sex differences—that is, if we can't escape some kind of story about gender—feminism is essential to challenging the meaning that humans today make of gender in patriarchy.

Feminism

In mainstream political discourse in the United States, patriarchy is not a term often used to describe contemporary society but instead is—if spoken of at all—reserved for assessments of the past. Most people will acknowledge that for most of U.S. history, women were either the property of men or, at best, second-class citizens, denied the rights of men in politics and virtually all arenas of life (though the depth of the dehumanization of women during that phase of patriarchy is often minimized, with illusions about how 'putting women up on a pedestal' benefited them).

If patriarchy is used in mainstream conversation about the contemporary world, it typically is applied only to the most conservative religious ideologies of male dominance, such as the Quiverfull Movement, which sees women's place as in the home, submitting to the divinely ordained rule of husbands and bearing children with no family planning or birth control.[48] Less extreme approaches, such as Promise Keepers,[49] connect men's quest to be good Christians with husbands taking their place as the natural head of the family in the divine plan, what some have called 'soft patriarchy'.[50] The man's job in a Christian household, in one popular formulation, is to be 'protector, provider, and pastor' to his wife and children. From this perspective, men are responsible for taking care of the family, which requires male dominance—patriarchy is therefore seen as positive.

But should we describe U.S. society today, in general, as patriarchal? As a result of the achievements of the suffragist and women's liberation movements in the nineteenth and twentieth centuries, women and girls now have opportunities in education, business, and politics that once were closed off. Doesn't the prominence of a politician such as Hillary Clinton

---

48 Kathryn Joyce, *Quiverfull: Inside the Christian Patriarchy Movement* (Boston: Beacon, 2009).

49 "PK History," Promise Keepers. <https://promisekeepers.org/pk-history>

50 Mary Stewart Van Leeuwen, "Servanthood or Soft Patriarchy? A Christian Feminist Looks at the Promise Keepers Movement," *Journal of Men's Studies*, 5:3 (1997). <http://www.cbeinternational.org/sites/default/files/pp112_7sosp.pdf>

in the twenty-first century demonstrate that the United States is no longer a patriarchal society? By that logic, we would also have to declare that Pakistan has transcended patriarchy because a woman, the late Prime Minister Benazir Bhutto, held the highest political office. But no one—inside or outside of Pakistan—makes such a claim, nor should we make such a claim about the United States.

Societies, and the systems that structure power in them, are not static, of course. We can acknowledge positive changes as a result of the struggle against institutionalized male dominance and still recognize patriarchy as the appropriate term to define the sex/gender system in the contemporary United States. Such an analysis is not unique to sex/gender; even with the significant achievements of the civil rights and nationalist movements of various non-white groups we can acknowledge that the United States remains a white-supremacist society in significant ways, even with the election of Barack Obama as president. We are no more 'post-patriarchal' than we are 'post-racial'.

Feminism remains a crucial element of any program for social justice today, which is why patriarchal forces attempt to eliminate or marginalize feminist ideas. It's not surprising that the gains made by the women's movement produced a backlash, with patriarchy adapting to changing conditions and reasserting its legitimacy. Sometimes the demonization of feminism has been literal, such as conservative Christian presidential candidate Pat Robertson's claim in a 1992 fund-raising letter: "The feminist agenda is not about equal rights for women. It is about a socialist, anti-family political movement that encourages women to leave their husbands, kill their children, practice witchcraft, destroy capitalism and become lesbians."[51] Conservative radio talk show host Rush Limbaugh popularized the political slur "feminazi" to describe what he called "any female who is intolerant of any point of view that challenges militant feminism,"[52] but the term actually serves to ridicule and discipline women who continue to challenge patriarchy. Susan Faludi's 1991 book on the backlash against feminism[53] charted how the anti-feminist campaign that emerged in the 1980s argued that women had achieved equality but it had made them miserable. So, rather than continuing the struggle against institutionalized male dominance, patriarchy's message to women was to go backward, not forward, and abandon the idea that institutionalized male dominance can be challenged.

We shouldn't be surprised that when women make gains in some arenas, such as education and business, men in patriarchy assert control in others, especially sexuality. Sociologist Kathleen Barry argued that in recent decades:

> [W]hen women achieve the potential for economic independence, men are threatened with loss of control over women as their legal and economic property in marriage. To regain control, patriarchal domination reconfigures around sex by producing a social and public condition of sexual subordination that follows women into the public world.[54]

---

51 Maralee Schwartz and Kenneth J. Cooper, "Equal Rights Initiative in Iowa Attacked," *Washington Post*, August 23, 1992. <https://www.washingtonpost.com/archive/politics/1992/08/23/equal-rights-initiative-in-iowa-attacked/f3e553a1-b768-449f-8d65-d096f9e318ee/>

52 Rush H. Limbaugh, *The Way Things Ought to Be* (New York: Pocket Books, 1992), p. 193.

53 Susan Faludi, *Backlash: The Undeclared War against American Women* (New York: Crown, 1991).

54 Kathleen Barry, *The Prostitution of Sexuality* (New York: New York University Press, 1995), p. 53.

But even with the backlash, feminism endures, moving in what are often described as 'waves'. In U.S. history, the first wave of feminism marks the nineteenth and early twentieth century movement that led to women winning the right to vote with passage of the Nineteenth Amendment to the U.S. Constitution in 1920. The second wave of feminism in the United States began in the 1960s, taking up issues such as sexuality, men's violence, family structures, the economy, and remaining forms of legal discrimination. A third wave of feminism[55] led by younger women beginning in the 1990s focused more on empowerment and individual choice. There's talk of a fourth wave,[56] sometimes defined by a commitment to the interpretation of feminism promoted in the transgender movement,[57] though the term is not widely used. More recent approaches to feminism that developed after the backlash, especially those focusing primarily on individual women's choices within existing systems as the crucial site of feminist struggle, seem to have detached from a deep critique of patriarchy, as I illustrate throughout this book.

Within these waves, there have been varying approaches to feminism, reflecting different theoretical frameworks and different practical concerns. Among the competing frameworks that emerged in the second wave were radical, Marxist, socialist, liberal, psychoanalytical, existential, postmodern, eco-feminism.[58] When non-white women challenged the predominantly white character of early second-

---

55 Leslie Heywood and Jennifer Drake, eds., *Third Wave Agenda: Being Feminist, Doing Feminism* (Minneapolis: University of Minnesota Press, 1997).

56 Jennifer Baumgardner, *F'em: Goo Goo, Gaga and Some Thoughts on Balls* (Berkeley, CA: Seal Press, 2011).

57 "Glossary," *The Transadvocate*. <http://www.transadvocate.com/glossary>

58 Rosemarie P. Tong, *Feminist Thought: A More Comprehensive Introduction* (Boulder, CO: Westview Press, 2013, 4th edition).

wave feminism, movements struggled to correct the distortions rooted in white supremacy, with varied success; some women of color choose to identify as womanist[59] rather than feminist. Lesbians challenged the predominantly heterosexual character of liberal feminism, and different feminisms went in varying directions as other challenges arose concerning everything from global politics to disability.

Rather than weigh the pros and cons of each approach, I will offer a summary of what I have learned from feminism.

As suggested in the chapter on sex/gender, because reproduction is not a trivial matter, the biological differences between male and female humans are not trivial, and it's plausible that these physical differences could give rise to meaningful intellectual, emotional, and moral differences between males and females. Though we know relatively little about how the basic biological differences influence those psychological capacities, the dominant culture routinely assumes that the effects are greater than have been established. Some even assert, figuratively speaking, that male and female humans are so different that we may as well be from different planets (the 'Men Are from Mars, Women Are from Venus' phenomenon[60]) or that, literally, there are distinctive male and female genomes so that male and females humans differ almost as much as humans differ from chimpanzees.[61]

In fact, male and female humans are much more similar than different.[62] A metasynthesis of studies showed small

---

59   Alice Walker, *In Search of Our Mothers' Gardens: Womanist Prose* (San Diego, CA: Harcourt Brace Jovanovich, 1983).

60   John Gray, *Men Are from Mars, Women Are from Venus* (New York: Harper-Collins, 1992).

61   For a critique, see Sarah S. Richardson, *Sex Itself: The Search for Male and Female in the Human Genome* (Chicago: University of Chicago Press, 2013).

62   Janet Shibley Hyde, "The Gender Similarity Hypothesis," *American Psychologist*, 60:6 (September 2005): 581–592.

differences and noted that problems in measurement may mean that even those differences are not significant.[63] Researchers have found that the perception of males and females as highly different is significantly associated with both hostile sexism ("an adversarial view of gender relations in which women are perceived as seeking control over men") and benevolent sexism ("a subjectively positive view of gender relations in which women are perceived as pure creatures who ought to be protected, supported, and adored; as necessary companions to make a man complete; but as weak and therefore best relegated to traditional gender roles").[64] In patriarchal societies based on gendered power, focus on the differences is used to rationalize disparities in power and the distribution of resources.

Challenging the patriarchal assumption that reproduction-based sex differences yield dramatic differences in other areas of life is at the core of feminism, as Jane Clare Jones points out:

> Feminism, as a political movement aimed at the liberation of women, has long theorized gender not as an innate essence, but as a hierarchical system enforcing women's subservience. Characterizing certain personality traits—compliance, nurturance, the desire to be pretty or objectified—as 'natural' to women, is, according to feminist analysis, a primary mechanism for maintaining gender hierarchy.[65]

Whatever one's position on what the differences in male and female biology may mean for intellectual, emotional, and moral

---

63 Ethan Zell, et al., "Evaluating Gender Similarities and Differences Using Metasynthesis," *American Psychologist*, 70:1 (January 2015): 10–20.

64 Ethan Zell, et al., "Mars, Venus, or Earth? Sexism and the Exaggeration of Psychological Gender Differences," *Sex Roles*, 2016. doi 10.1007/s11199-016-0622-1

65 Jane Clare Jones, "'You Are Killing Me': On Hate Speech and Feminist Silencing," *Trouble and Strife*, May 16, 2015. <http://www.troubleandstrife.org/new-articles/you-are-killing-me/>

differences, there is no evidence that any of those potential differences are significant in determining the political status of men and women. Whatever the conflicting views (between feminists and non-feminists, and among different styles of feminism) about the meaning of the differences between males and females, this much is uncontroversial in feminism, and in most of the contemporary United States: Women should be full citizens. If we take that claim seriously, we should remove barriers to full participation in other arenas—culture, education, theology, economics, the family, personal relationships—since those inequalities will impede women's ability to exercise full citizenship.

Just as winning the right to vote didn't magically eliminate all other barriers created by white supremacy for non-white people, women's suffrage didn't magically eliminate all patriarchal barriers. Some of these issues involve the law, or can be addressed through law, but many of them are so deeply woven into the fabric of society that a radical transformation is necessary, not only in policies and institutions but in how we understand what it means to be male and female, and human.

Based on my experience and reading of relevant research, many of the critiques offered by second-wave feminists continue to provide the most compelling way to understand the enduring power of patriarchy. U.S. society has changed over recent decades—women now vie for top political offices and serve in positions of power, albeit not in numbers proportionate to the population and typically only if they accept other hierarchies, especially in international affairs and economics—but on some issues we have lost ground, such as the expansion and wide acceptance of the sexual-exploitation industries (prostitution and pornography). Today, the domination/subordination dynamic of patriarchy remains firmly in place, with institutionalized male dominance ceding ground on some issues but holding the line in other places. If I have to choose a label for the feminism in which I root my own teaching, political organizing, and personal life, it would be radical feminism.

By radical feminist, I mean, first, the understanding that men's subordination of women is a product of patriarchy and that the ultimate goal of feminism is the end of patriarchy's gender-as-hierarchy system, not merely liberal accommodation within the system. Second, radical feminism is central to challenging the larger problem of hierarchy and the domination/subordination dynamics in other arenas of human life; while not sufficient by itself, the end of patriarchy is a necessary condition for liberation more generally.

One of the most insightful—and controversial—radical feminists, the late writer Andrea Dworkin,[66] was central to the feminist anti-pornography movement that was my introduction to this radical feminism. The feminist philosophy that has shaped my thinking has been articulated most clearly by Marilyn Frye;[67] Catharine MacKinnon[68] has been influential in my understanding of the law's role; Gerda Lerner helped me understand the relationship between gender and class; and Audre Lorde[69] and Barbara Smith[70] challenged many of my unconscious assumptions about gender and race.

Important to the struggle to bring to feminist theory and politics a deeper analysis of the complexity of all these

---

66 Andrea Dworkin, *Heartbreak: The Political Memoir of a Feminist Militant* (New York: Basic Books, 2002).

67 Marilyn Frye, *The Politics of Reality* (Freedom, CA: Crossing Press, 1983).

68 Catharine A. MacKinnon, *Feminism Unmodified: Discourses on Life and Law* (Cambridge, MA: Harvard University Press, 1987).

69 Audre Lorde, *Sister Outsider* (Freedom, CA: Crossing Press, 1984).

70 Barbara Smith, *The Truth That Never Hurts: Writings on Race, Gender, and Freedom* (New Brunswick, NJ: Rutgers University Press, 2000).

interactions among systems of power has been Patricia Hill Collins' 1990 book on black feminist thought and "the matrix of domination."[71] Other sources of my early understanding of these themes were the work of bell hooks, especially her 1984 book[72] and her ongoing critique of "white-supremacist capitalist patriarchy," and the influential 1981 collection *This Bridge Called My Back: Writing by Radical Women of Color.*[73]

Today there's a broad consensus within all varieties of feminism that intellectual and political work must be 'intersectional', a term from a 1989 article by Kimberlé Crenshaw[74] about how black women could be marginalized by movements for both racial and gender justice when their concerns did not conform to either group's ideology or strategy. Crenshaw has described intersectionality as "an analytic sensibility, a way of thinking about identity and its relationship to power,"[75] and the term is now used to talk about not only gender and race but other systems that turn difference into discrimination and dominance. While the term is relatively new, the analysis and spirit behind it go back further. For example, Florynce Kennedy, a prominent attorney and activist in the feminist and civil rights movements, in 1976 referred to the United States as "a pathologically, institutionally racist,

---

71 Patricia Hill Collins, *Black Feminist Thought: Knowledge, Consciousness, and the Politics of Empowerment* (New York: Routledge Classics, 2008).

72 bell hooks, *Feminist Theory: From Margin to Center* (Boston: South End Press, 1984).

73 Cherríe Moraga and Gloria E. Anzaldúa, eds, *This Bridge Called My Back: Writing by Radical Women of Color* (Albany, NY: State University of New York Press, 2015, 4th edition).

74 Kimberlé Crenshaw, "Demarginalizing the Intersection of Race and Sex: A Black Feminist Critique of Antidiscrimination Doctrine, Feminist Theory and Antiracist Politics," *University of Chicago Legal Forum*, 1 (1989): 139–167.

75 Kimberlé Crenshaw, "Why intersectionality can't wait," *Washington Post*, September 24, 2015. <https://www.washingtonpost.com/news/in-theory/wp/2015/09/24/why-intersectionality-cant-wait/>

sexist, classist society."[76] The statement of the Combahee River Collective, a group of black lesbian feminists in the late 1970s, named not only sexism and racism but also capitalism and imperialism as forces constraining their lives:

> The most general statement of our politics at the present time would be that we are actively committed to struggling against racial, sexual, heterosexual, and class oppression, and see as our particular task the development of integrated analysis and practice based upon the fact that the major systems of oppression are interlocking. The synthesis of these oppressions creates the conditions of our lives.[77]

The collective's statement identifies "sexual oppression as a constant factor in our day-to-day existence":

> As children we realized that we were different from boys and that we were treated differently. For example, we were told in the same breath to be quiet both for the sake of being 'ladylike' and to make us less objectionable in the eyes of white people. As we grew older we became aware of the threat of physical and sexual abuse by men.[78]

A contemporary example of intersectionality is Monique Morris' analysis, drawing on interviews with young African American women, explaining why black girls are expelled from New York schools at fifty-three times the rate of white girls: Black girls' appearance, speech, and actions are often perceived

---

76 Sherie M. Randolph, *Florynce "Flo" Kennedy: The Life of a Radical Black Feminist* (Chapel Hill: University of North Carolina Press, 2015), p. 1.

77 Combahee River Collective, "The Combahee River Collective Statement," in Barbara Smith, ed., *Home Girls: A Black Feminist Anthology* (New York: Kitchen Table/Women of Color Press, 1983; New Brunswick, NJ: Rutgers University Press, 2000), p. 264.

78 *Ibid.*, p. 266.

as 'delinquent' due to assumptions about black femininity that are based on race, sex/gender, and class biases.[79]

Another example: Research has demonstrated that women's routine, persistent experiences of being sexually objectified can lead to heightened concerns about their physical safety because such experiences carry an implicit threat of rape. In a patriarchal society, that is not surprising. In a white-supremacist society, in which non-white women are valued less than white women in most settings, it also should not be surprising that African American women report a greater number of sexual objectification experiences and a greater fear of crime than white women.[80]

Intersectional approaches like these help us better understand the complex results of what radical feminists argue is a central feature of patriarchy: Men's relentless efforts to control women's sexuality and reproduction. As Frye puts it:

> For females to be subordinated and subjugated to males on a global scale, and for males to organize themselves and each other as they do, billions of female individuals, virtually all who see life on this planet, must be reduced to a more-or-less willing toleration of subordination and servitude to men. The primary sites of this reduction are the sites of heterosexual relation and encounter—courtship and marriage-arrangement, romance, sexual liaisons, fucking, marriage, prostitution, the normative family, incest and child sexual assault. It is on this terrain of

---

79 Monique W. Morris, *Pushout: The Criminalization of Black Girls in Schools* (New York: New Press, 2016). See also Kimberlé Williams Crenshaw, with Priscilla Ocen and Jyoti Nanda, "Black Girls Matter: Pushed Out, Overpoliced and Underprotected," African American Policy Forum, and Center for Intersectionality and Social Policy Studies, 2015. <http://www.law.columbia.edu/null/download?&exclusive=filemgr.download&file_id=613546>

80 Laurel B. Watson, et al., "Understanding the Relationships Among White and African American Women's Sexual Objectification Experiences, Physical Safety Anxiety, and Psychological Distress," *Sex Roles*, 72:3 (2015): 91–104.

heterosexual connection that girls and women are habituated to abuse, insult, degradation, that girls are reduced to women—to wives, to whores, to mistresses, to sex slaves, to clerical workers and textile workers, to the mothers of men's children.[81]

To make that claim is not to suggest that every man treats every woman as a sex slave—each individual man in patriarchy is not at every moment actively engaged in the oppression of women, but men routinely act in ways that perpetuate patriarchy and harm women. It's also true that patriarchy's obsession with hierarchy, including an often harsh system of ranking men, means that most men lose out in the game to acquire significant wealth and power. Complex systems produce complicated results, and still there are identifiable patterns: Patriarchy is a system that delivers material benefits to men—unequally depending on men's other attributes (such as race, class, sexual orientation, nationality, immigration status) and on men's willingness to adapt to patriarchal values—but patriarchy constrains *all* women. The physical, psychological, and spiritual suffering endured by women varies widely, again depending on other attributes and sometimes just on the luck of the draw, but no woman escapes some level of that suffering. And at the core of that system is men's control of women's sexuality and reproduction:

> Without (hetero)sexual abuse, (hetero)sexual harassment and the (hetero)sexualization of every aspect of female bodies and behaviors, there would not be patriarchy, and whatever other forms or materializations of oppression might exist, they would not have the shapes, boundaries and dynamics of the racism, nationalism, and so on that we are so familiar with.[82]

---

81   Frye, *Willful Virgin*, p. 130.
82   *Ibid.*

The radical feminists I have worked with do not limit their critique to patriarchy. To emphasize the *radical* potential of radical feminism: Beyond the sex/gender system, radical feminism's understanding of the way in which patriarchy normalizes hierarchy leads not just to a focus on men's domination of women but also to a deeper critique of power systems more generally. While feminism focuses on challenging institutionalized male dominance, a feminist analysis identifies how patriarchal societies tend to treat all relationships as a site of struggle for domination. In patriarchy, hierarchy is understood as an immutable reality—the belief that the ordering of human relationships should, and always will be, based on power. Yet hierarchies are inconsistent with human flourishing unless a compelling argument can be made that the hierarchy is necessary to help those with less power in the system, a test that can rarely be met. Feminism is not the only way into a broader critique of the many types of oppression, of course, but it is one important way, and was for me the first route into such a framework.

The various inequalities that define the contemporary world—imposed through white supremacy, imperialism, capitalism—all are based on this central feature of patriarchy, an attempt to make the domination/subordination dynamic appear to be a natural, and hence inevitable, feature of human societies. All of these systems have their own histories and contemporary practices, and they interact in complex ways. At any given moment, one or more of those systems of inequality might be most salient to specific individuals, most relevant to shaping their social experience. But all those systems are based on the same domination/subordination dynamic.

In the past three decades, radical feminism has lost ground to traditional liberal feminism and various expressions of third/fourth-wave feminism, which I would describe as simply liberal feminism with a younger aesthetic and rhetoric. Even when feminists from these various camps can agree on a policy—for example, defending abortion and reproductive rights—there will be variations in underlying philosophy; in the rationale for the policy; in strategy and tactics for political organizing; and in personal and rhetorical styles. In any healthy political movement seeking to change the distribution of wealth and power there will be disagreements, and feminism is no different—intra-feminist debates can get heated.

In the following chapters on specific issues, I'll explore this tension in greater detail but for now want to pose a simple question: If radical feminism continues to be such a compelling way to understand sex/gender in the contemporary world, as I am arguing, why has it been so marginalized, not only in the culture at large but also within feminism and women's studies? My answer: Precisely because this perspective is compelling, and hence challenging; a serious commitment to a radical approach requires significant changes in all our lives, whether male or female. Radical feminism asks us to investigate not only how patriarchy has structured the institutions in which we work and live, but also the way it has structured our own sense of ourselves, how it has defined our own imaginations. In my experience, taking seriously that project is not only difficult but often can feel overwhelming. It demands a lifetime of critical self-reflection, which can be painful. It asks us, borrowing from James Baldwin, not to run away from patriarchy but to walk toward it, so that at least we know what is hitting us.

PRESSING
ARGUMENTS

The older I get, the more I have become aware of (1) the complexity of the world and (2) the limits of human knowledge in our quest to understand the world. As a result, I've become less interested in ideological systems that claim to have it all worked out and in the dogma those ideological systems generate.

At the same time, I have become (1) more aware of the abusive and oppressive effects of the concentration of wealth and power, and hence (2) more eager than ever to figure out how power works in the world to increase our effectiveness in challenging those illegitimate concentrations of wealth and power. When I think I have some piece of this puzzle figured out, more than ever I feel obligated to act on it.

Balancing those two instincts—intellectual humility and a sense of moral urgency to act—is hardly a new problem. Everyone is susceptible to ideological arrogance ("I have figured out the answer, and you should follow me") and political passivity ("It's all too complicated for me to know what to do, and so I'll do nothing"), and history is littered with reminders of how often people get it wrong. Honest self-reflection should lead us to see our own mistakes; in my life, I've failed on both ends of the spectrum.

In this section, I want to try to work out the balance in the context of three contemporary issues that are controversial not only in the dominant culture but within feminism—rape and sexual intrusion, prostitution and pornography, and the biological and political claims of the transgender movement. Over the years, many people have told me that they do their best to avoid confrontations around these issues, in part because the conflicts can be so emotionally draining and in part to prevent rifts within their political and social networks. At times, I have avoided one or more of these questions for similar reasons, but the older I get the more I feel obligated to be part of the conversation, in part because of my privilege.

That may, once again, seem counterintuitive. If I am critical of systems that give me unearned power and status, why would I want to speak with the privilege that comes from those systems? Over the years many people more vulnerable than I am, in professional or personal terms, have encouraged me to use my job security (a tenured professor) and social status (white guy in the United States) to articulate these analyses. On all three of these issues, women have told me privately that they hold positions that draw criticism from other feminists and don't always feel free to make these arguments. Some fear risking funding for the agency they worked for, while others don't want to be ostracized in their social circles.

To be clear: I do not claim to be speaking on behalf of those women, or any women, nor am I looking for a talisman to ward off challenges. I not only expect criticism but encourage substantive responses. But these conversations with feminist women who are afraid to speak their minds, not only in public but even in some feminist spaces, suggest a need for more critical self-reflection on how feminism, and the left more generally—as intellectual projects and political movements—have reached this point. Why do people feel they have to silence themselves about crucial questions in feminist/ progressive spaces, which are supposed to be committed to critical thinking about power?

With that question in the background, I return to this basic human predicament: We rarely know enough to know for sure. Even with extensive research and insightful analyses that might give us clarity in offering policy proposals to respond to illegitimate wealth and power, we frequently lack the capacity to predict the consequences of those policies. That is, even when we are right about the problem, we often are fumbling around in the dark when we propose responses and remedies. This reminder of our intellectual limits has led me to ask a basic question whenever I encounter a new idea, political project, or policy proposal:

"Is this likely to help people create and maintain stable, decent human communities that can remain in a sustainable relationship with the larger living world?"

Even when I have to make a judgment based on incomplete evidence and with inadequate analytic clarity, this question helps guide me in making my best guess about actions I might take or endorse. The question doesn't demand certainty but simply asks whether this proposed step is likely to put us on a productive path. A focus on 'human communities' signals that my concern is not exclusively on individual rights but on the recognition that such rights depend on an underlying collective social health. By focusing on 'stable' and 'decent', I recognize that tradition has a role in human life (the stability that comes with tradition matters), but that all traditions have to be tested against moral principles (being decent to one another matters, too, and traditions can become a rationalization for injustice).

And including a recognition of the 'larger living world' beyond the human family reminds us that social justice and ecological sustainability have to go forward together if there is to be a human future on the planet.

All of my research and experience tells me that any idea, project, or proposal involving sex/gender that is going to meet those criteria must be willing to name patriarchy as a target. At the risk of annoying repetition, I do not know how a movement for sex/gender justice can make progress without grappling with patriarchy, its hierarchy, and the resulting domination/subordination dynamic. This is not a matter of mere semantics. Cynthia Cockburn reminds us that patriarchy

> is not merely a colourful term used by feminists to rebuke men. It is not a thing of bygone days, nor a rhetorical flourish. It is an important dimension of the structuring of modern societies, whether capitalist or state socialist. It is a living reality, a system that quite observably shapes the lives and differentiates the chances of women and of men. The struggle for sex equality, however innocently it may present itself, is an attempt to contradict, to undo, patriarchy.[83]

In the previous chapter, I argued that the radical feminist tradition offered the most compelling path to undoing patriarchy, but I acknowledged that the radical position is marginalized, not only in the dominant culture but within feminism. Of the other feminist approaches, which are most central to the conversation today? In the political discourse of the dominant culture, to the degree that feminism is visible, it's most likely a liberal approach that focuses on gaining equality for women within existing political, legal, and economic

---

83 Cynthia Cockburn, *In the Way of Women: Men's Resistance to Sex Equality in Organizations* (Cornell, NY: ILR Press, 1991), p. 18.

institutions.[84] In academic circles, feminists continue to pursue a variety of different theoretical frameworks, but to the degree there is a dominant feminist perspective, it is postmodern in character.[85] That position, while famously difficult to define, challenges the stability and coherence not only of existing institutions but of the very concepts that we use within them, and tends to focus on language and performance as key to identity and experience.

These two approaches, liberalism and postmodernism, come out of very different sets of assumptions, but are similar in their practical commitment to individualism in politics. That assessment paints with a broad brush, of course, but in my experience, liberal and postmodern feminists find it relatively easy to come together on policy options because of a tendency to evaluate a proposal based on whether it maximizes choices for individual women rather than whether it resists patriarchy's hierarchy and challenges the power of men as a class. For liberals, the political category of women is relatively stable but the solutions are centered on the rights claimed by individuals. For postmoderns, the category 'women' is often in scare-quotes to emphasize its instability, and hence solutions will inevitably center on the rights claims of individuals.

Even when liberals and postmoderns acknowledge the deeply patriarchal nature of the contemporary world, they often do not focus on the system, either for pragmatic or theoretical reasons. Liberals valorize working within the system; postmoderns seem to argue that we can transcend the

---

84 The book most often associated with the emergence of second-wave liberal feminism is Betty Friedan, *The Feminine Mystique* (New York: W.W. Norton and Co., 1963).

85 The book typically cited as central to a postmodern feminist approach is Judith Butler, *Gender Trouble: Feminism and the Subversion of Identity* (New York: Routledge, 1990).

system through language and performance. Liberalism is self-consciously committed to individualism; the category 'women' exists, but progress is made by focusing on individual women. Postmodernism is simply liberalism to the Nth degree; if a stable category 'women' can't exist, any remedies based on it are questionable. Many postmodern feminists have radical politics on a variety of subjects—such as critiques of the systems of white supremacy, imperialism, and capitalism—but they do not adopt a radical feminist analysis.[86]

That is a blunt assessment of liberal and postmodern feminism, but one that I believe is supported by the debates over the issues I examine here. I am not denying the complexity of these competing philosophies but rather identifying patterns I have observed. I am not trashing feminists who identify with the liberal or postmodern traditions, and I have been a friendly colleague of people in those traditions and worked on projects with them.

I also am not defending every claim ever made under the umbrella of radical feminism, nor agreeing with every strategic decision ever made by radical feminists. Like any intellectual/political perspective, there is debate and disagreement, and differences in style and tone among people who identify with the perspective. I have met some liberal feminists I find easier to engage than some radical feminists. I have met some postmodern feminists I enjoy talking with, even though I'm often not sure that I understand their jargon. In other words, the considerable variation in the human species shows up everywhere, including feminism.

A friend once told me that he thought that most people approached intellectual and political life as if they were joining

---

86   For a thorough analysis of postmodern feminism from a radical feminist perspective, see Diane Bell and Renate Klein, eds., *Radically Speaking: Feminism Reclaimed* (North Melbourne, Australia: Spinifex Press, 1996).

a street gang, deciding which colors to wear. Perhaps it's inevitable that we seek meaning in our lives through group membership, and that membership helps us find within ourselves the strength to act, and that this requires a certain amount of conformity to the group's party line—even when the group is supposed to be dedicated to challenging conformity to social norms. I can see points in my life where I made that choice, and at times that conformity hindered my ability to analyze the world accurately.

To avoid such intellectual rigidity, some people claim to reject membership in any group and evaluate every question on its own merits, which produces a different kind of absurdity. No knowledge claim is pre-theoretical; that is, we always have some ideas about how the world works—stated or unstated—when we investigate the world. Pretending to be a free agent without intellectual or political commitments is a kind of willed ignorance about how human inquiry proceeds, which tends to dull people's ability to question their own assumptions. People who express disdain for others' street gangs inevitably belong to one of the privileged gangs in the dominant culture.

As we try to understand the patterns in human affairs, we construct social theory (using the term 'theory' here to describe a framework for analysis that cannot claim the potential predictive capacity of scientific theory) to articulate our understanding of how power operates, and we also should stay in dynamic tension with such theory, recognizing the limits of our understanding. Andrea Dworkin captured this need for critical self-reflection:

> The purpose of theory is to clarify the world in which we live, how it works, why things happen as they do. The purpose of theory is understanding. Understanding is energizing. It energizes to action. When theory becomes an impediment to action, it is time to discard the theory and return naked [as one can be], that

is, without theory, to the world of reality. People become slaves to theory because people are used to meeting expectations they have not originated—to doing what they are told, to having everything mapped out, to having reality prepackaged. People can have an antiauthoritarian intention and yet function in a way totally consonant with the demands of authority. The deepest struggle is to root out of us and the institutions in which we participate the requirement that we slavishly conform. But an adherence to ideology, to any ideology, can give us the grand illusion of freedom when in fact we are being manipulated and used by those whom the theory serves. The struggle for freedom has to be a struggle toward integrity defined in every possible sphere of reality—sexual integrity, economic integrity, psychological integrity, integrity of expression, integrity of faith and loyalty and heart. Anything that shortcuts us away from viewing integrity as an essential goal or anything that diverts our attention from integrity as a revolutionary value serves only to reinforce the authoritarian values of the world in which we live.[87]

So, I continue to identify with radical feminism because the assumptions and conclusions of writers and activists in that tradition continue to be the most compelling ways to understand the sex/gender system, but I try to cultivate a spirit of open inquiry. My goal is not to say "this is what radical feminism is" but rather explain why I find the radical feminist tradition central to my intellectual and political life.

To say women and men make up identifiable, coherent classes for political analysis is not to say all women and all men are the same. Nor does that claim depend on an assertion that any idea, political project, or policy proposal will affect all women and men in the same way, or that outcomes will be evaluated the same way by all women and men. Radical

---

87 Andrea Dworkin, *Letters from a War Zone* (Brooklyn, NY: Lawrence Hill Books, 1993), pp. 127–128.

feminism need not be totalizing or essentialist when it observes patterns in how female humans are treated in systems based on institutionalized male dominance, or when it seeks remedies that take those patterns seriously.

The term 'radical' also does not mean that the only acceptable remedy is revolution; radical feminists can, and often do, pursue gradual change through reform, but reform with a radical analysis and revolutionary spirit. The discussion of the issues that follows will make it clear why I believe radical feminism offers the best way to understand and respond to patriarchy.

One last reminder: I speak for myself—I'm not presenting the definitive version of any set of ideas but rather the version of these ideas that makes sense and works for me. By 'works for me' I do not mean in purely intellectual or political terms, but also personally. The ideas I present here have helped me understand how I was socialized in patriarchy into a toxic masculinity that not only subordinates women but also crippled my own capacity to be fully human.

In my early struggles with loneliness and alienation from masculinity in patriarchy, I thought the task was to 'get in touch with my feminine side' to balance the masculine. But without a feminist critique, accepting that framework still left me trapped within the domination/subordination dynamic, which is how masculinity and femininity are shaped in patriarchy. Feminism taught me how to analyze that dynamic rather than capitulate to it. Feminism, I came to understand, was not a threat to men but a gift to us.

RAPE AND
RAPE CULTURE:
'NORMAL' VIOLENCE

In patriarchy, in the United States, some folks still want to believe that ...

Rape is a rare occurrence, and the few real sexual assaults that are committed are perpetrated by deviant men who can be handled in the criminal justice system and through psychological treatment. Men do not rape women they know socially, husbands do not rape their wives, and male bosses do not sexually exploit female employees—whatever happens in those relationships is just the way things sometimes play out between men and women.

Those statements summarize the dominant culture's view of sexual aggression and abuse before 1970. After that, feminists pressed the culture to give up the illusion of rape-as-deviance and recognize that the commonplace nature of men's domination-through-sexuality demands a deeper analysis. The concepts of date rape, marital rape, and sexual harassment were developed to name aggression and exploitation that had been invisible, not only to the legal system but to most of society.

This struggle over the social and legal understanding of rape is not a new phenomenon in U.S. history. Estelle Freeman points out that, going back to the nineteenth century, "Generations of women's rights and racial justice advocates have contested the narrow understanding of rape as a brutal attack on a chaste, unmarried, white woman by a stranger, typically portrayed as an African American man."[88] The second-wave feminist critique of rape continued this challenge to the patriarchal and white-supremacist politics of rape, articulated by Susan Griffin in a 1971 magazine article ("rape is a form of mass terrorism, for the victims of rape are chosen indiscriminately, but the propagandists for male supremacy broadcast that it is women who cause rape by being unchaste or in the wrong place at the wrong time—in essence, by behaving as though they were free" and "rape is not an isolated act that can be rooted out from patriarchy without ending patriarchy itself"[89]) and in the often-quoted assertion from Susan Brownmiller's 1975 book, that rape "is nothing more or less than a conscious process of intimidation by which all men keep all women in a state of fear."[90]

Out of these kinds of feminist analyses of men's violence in patriarchy came organizing for rape crisis centers and domestic violence shelters to help victims; legal reforms intended to make criminal prosecutions and civil remedies more effective; and feminist education and advocacy programs aimed at reducing

---

88   Estelle B. Freedman, *Redefining Rape: Sexual Violence in the Era of Suffrage and Segregation* (Cambridge, MA: Harvard University Press, 2013), p. 1.

89   Susan Griffin, "Rape: The All-American Crime," *Ramparts Magazine*, September 1971, p. 35.

90   Susan Brownmiller, *Against Our Will: Men, Women and Rape* (New York: Ballantine, 1975), p. 15.

rates of violence.[91] None of those measures magically solved the problems, but without feminism none of those changes would have happened. Grudgingly, the dominant culture has accepted an attenuated version of the feminist analysis and slowly acknowledged the need for services, reform, and education. But mainstream institutions have diluted the power of that radical analysis, and in recent years even some within the anti-violence movement have pushed a feminist analysis to the margins.

The patriarchal social system of the contemporary United States has never been able to come to terms with the *disturbing insight of radical feminism: Rape is normal.* Not normal in the sense of 'good' (a social norm that we should uphold) or 'inevitable' (a product of biology that therefore can't be changed) but normal in two other ways: (1) Women's experiences of men's sexual aggression are so common as to be statistically normal—that is, it happens to most women; and (2) these patterns indicate that the behaviors are an expression of the underlying sex/gender norms of the culture, not violations of those norms—that is, the culture does not openly endorse rape but does endorse a patriarchal conception of masculinity/ femininity that invites men to be sexually aggressive.

Statistics

Rape is a vastly underreported crime; most women who are raped do not go to law enforcement agencies, and therefore crime statistics tell us little about the prevalence of rape. But the feminist movement's activism against men's violence led to

---

91 Freedman, *Redefining Rape*, Chapter 14, "The Enduring Politics of Rape," pp. 271–289.

research based on women's experiences rather than on crime reporting, and those studies have found varying rates of rape and other forms of assault.

On a global scale, 30% of women over the age of fifteen have experienced "intimate partner violence," defined as physical, sexual, or emotional violence, based on data from eighty-one countries. The rate in North America is 21%.[92]

For many years, anti-rape activists in the United States cited the statistic that one in three girls is sexually abused and that 38% of the women reported sexual abuse before age eighteen.[93] A recent review of the data by researchers concluded that in the United States, at least one of every six women has been raped at some time in her life, a figure that is now widely accepted.[94] Much of this sexual violence is directed at young people; in the National Violence Against Women Survey, slightly more than half of the 14.8% of women who reported being raped said it happened before age eighteen.[95]

Those statistics address acts that meet the legal definition of rape, but women and girls face a much broader range of what we can call 'sexual intrusions', sexual acts that they do not request and do not want but experience regularly—sexually corrosive text messages and calls, cyberbullying, sexual taunting on the

---

92 K.M. Devries, et al., "The Global Prevalence of Intimate Partner Violence Against Women," *Science*, 340:6140 (June 28, 2013): 1527–1528.

93 Diana E.H. Russell, *Sexual Exploitation: Rape, Child Sexual Abuse, and Workplace Harassment* (Beverly Hills, CA: Sage, 1984), pp. 285–286.

94 Patricia Tjaden and Nancy Thoennes, *Extent, Nature, and Consequences of Rape Victimization: Findings from the National Violence Against Women Survey* (Washington, DC: U.S. Department of Justice/National Institute of Justice, 2006). <http://www.ncjrs.gov/pdffiles1/nij/210346.pdf>

95 Patricia Tjaden and Nancy Thoennes, *Full Report of the Prevalence, Incidence, and Consequences of Violence Against Women: Findings from the National Violence Against Women Survey* (Washington, DC: U.S. Department of Justice/National Institute of Justice, 2000). <https://www.ncjrs.gov/pdffiles1/nij/183781.pdf>

streets, sexual harassment in schools and workplaces, coercive sexual pressure in dating, sexual assault, and violence that is sexualized. In public lectures on these issues, I list these categories and women's heads nod, an affirmation of the routine nature of men's sexual and sexualized intrusions into their daily lives. I sometimes tell audiences that I have just completed an extensive study and found that the percentage of women in the United States who have experienced some form of sexual intrusion is 100%. Women understand the bleak humor—no study is necessary to confirm something so routine.

If we describe rape as "sexually invasive dehumanization"[96] to capture the distinctive nature of the crime, then let's ask this difficult question: How much of everyday life do women experience as sexually invasive dehumanization on some level? This "cumulative impact of living with sexism" is often unexamined, according to Jessica Valenti:

> Walking on the street, tweeting, working—just living—while female shapes who we are and who we think we can be. When a high school teacher asked me on a date just a few days after I graduated, I wasn't traumatized. The day that an ex-boyfriend taped a used condom to my dorm-room door, scrawling 'whore' across the dry-erase board, didn't forever damage me. When I receive a rape threat via email, my life's trajectory does not shift. But it would be silly to believe that who I am today isn't in part created by the distinct combination of those moments.[97]

This doesn't mean all women are accosted every day, of course. But can this dehumanization become so 'normal' that

---

96 Michelle J. Anderson, "All-American Rape," *St. John's Law Review*, 79:3 (2012): 643.

97 Jessica Valenti, "What Does a Lifetime of Leers Do to Us?" *New York Times*, June 4, 2016. <http://www.nytimes.com/2016/06/05/opinion/sunday/what-does-a-lifetime-of-leers-do-to-us.html?_r=0>

it is difficult to recognize our collective capitulation to the underlying norms? Here's one story about normalized sexually invasive dehumanization:

After a class in which the subject of sexism and sexual violence had come up, two first-year students linger to talk with me. Both have pledged a sorority at the University of Texas, and they want to discuss the sexual politics of that social system. I ask whether they ever talk among themselves about the sexual threats they face at fraternity parties. They look at me with that "adults are so out of touch" expression and say that of course they understand the risks and are aware of the 'tricks' that fraternity men use at parties, especially the endless flow of alcohol.[98] "But we have a strategy," they tell me. "We always go to those parties as a group, and we never leave anyone behind."

I pause to consider the appropriate response from an older male professor, wanting to be honest but not overly critical. I tell them that the only other context in which I have heard the phrase "we never leave anyone behind" is the military. "In your social lives, you have adopted a rule that soldiers use to express their commitment to each other in war," I say. "At parties where you are supposed to be having fun, you have to act as if you are on a battlefield."

I do not enjoy saying that, they do not enjoy hearing it, and we are all quiet for a moment. It is important, but not always easy, to recognize what is 'normal' in our culture.

---

98 Some fraternity members refer to these tactics as "working out a yes." See Peggy Reeves Sanday, *Fraternity Gang Rape: Sex, Brotherhood, and Privilege on Campus* (New York: New York University Press, 1990).

Sex/Gender Norms

Why do those young women have to treat a fraternity party as a battlefield? If the answer is not that all the men in fraternities are deviant psychopaths who want to hurt women—which clearly is not the case—then the question leads us to examine how 'normal' boys and men are socialized in the United States. As with any other social question, there is no single answer that applies to everyone; again, we search for patterns in socialization to help explain patterns in behavior. From the research available and my own experience, here is the pattern I see, and have experienced:

Men generally are trained through a variety of cultural institutions to view sex as the acquisition of pleasure by the taking of women. Sex is a sphere in which men are trained to see themselves as naturally dominant. Throughout the culture, women are objectified and women's sexuality is commodified. Sexual interactions are most sexy when men are dominant and women are subordinate; power is eroticized. Boys and men are told all this is natural, just the way things are—and always have been—between men and women.

In a patriarchal culture in which many men understand sex as the taking of pleasure from women, rape is an expression of the sexual norms of the culture, not a violation of those norms. Rape is both nominally illegal and completely normal at the same time, which is why men often do not view their own sexually aggressive or violent behavior as aggression or violence—to them, it's just sex. That's why some men who commit rape often also condemn rape, which they see as something other men do.

Feminist research into, and women's reflection upon, experiences of sexual violence indicate that rape involves the sexualization of power, the fusing in men's imaginations of sexual pleasure with domination and control. But the common phrase 'rape is about power, not sex' is misleading; rape is about the fusion of sex and domination, about the eroticization of control. When we are stuck in "an endless debate over whether rape is about sexual gratification on the one hand, or a display of power and dominance on the other; sex accomplished violently, or violence accomplished sexually,"[99] as one writer puts it, we obscure the uncomfortable reality that in patriarchy the two are intertwined, not just in rape but in much of 'normal' sexual activity. Yes, men who rape seek a sense of power, but men also use their power to get sex from women, sometimes under conditions that are not legally defined as rape but involve varying levels of control and coercion.

If this analysis seems far-fetched, think about the ways men in all-male spaces often talk about sex with women, such as asking each other, "Did you get any?" From that perspective, sex is the acquisition of pleasure from a woman, something one takes from a woman, and men talk openly among themselves about strategies to enhance the likelihood of 'getting some', even in the face of resistance from women. I remember that phrase from the high-school locker room, along with the strategies for getting sex that boys discussed. It didn't matter that I was a short, thin, effeminate boy who wasn't getting any and wasn't eager to be in sexual situations that intense—I was being socialized, learning what it meant to be a man having (or, at least, seeking to have) sex.

The words and phrases that men, and sometimes women, use to talk about sex make it hard to avoid a feminist analysis. Start with the most common slang term for sexual intercourse, 'fuck'. In other contexts, the word can suggest aggressive and/

---

99   Raymond M. Douglas, *On Being Raped* (Boston: Beacon, 2016), p. 66.

or immoral actions to win a victory in a business interaction ("I really fucked him over on that deal"); physical violence against an adversary ("We got in a fight and I fucked him up"); or the desire to dominate when hurled as a simple insult ("fuck you, buddy"). We live in a world in which people use the same word for sexual intercourse/interaction/intimacy and aggression/violence/domination, and then resist the notion that sex is routinely aggressive, claim to be outraged when sex becomes overtly violent, and feign surprise when feminists argue that men's violence is rooted in gendered norms of domination.

When I was a high school student, the phrase 'fuck or fight' was dispensed as advice: If you wanted to have sex with a girl, drive out on a deserted country road on a date, turn off the engine, put your car keys in your pocket, and tell her, 'fuck or fight'. I don't recall any classmate ever recoiling in horror from the joke; instead, we all laughed. I also remember laughing when boys reminded each other not to get too emotionally involved with girls by stating the goal was to "find 'em, feel 'em, fuck 'em, and forget 'em." This bravado masked tremendous insecurity, of course, but it indicates that we understood masculinity as demanding that we hide that insecurity and cover our fear by bonding around imagining the sexual use and abuse of women.

I'm not in locker rooms much these days and rarely in any all-male setting where such banter might be traded, and as a result my street slang is a bit outdated. So, I was taken aback when watching a recent Hollywood movie in which one man asked another, in reference to a conventionally attractive woman, "Are you hitting that?" Men today think nothing of inquiring about whether another man is in a sexual relationship with a woman by asking, "Are you hitting that?" The verb is aggressive, and the object is an object, not a person.

All of this, and much more, is what feminists mean when they describe the contemporary United States as a 'rape culture'. If it's still not clear, here's an exercise:

In your mind, line up six women you know—friends, family members, colleagues, neighbors, or just the women ahead of you in the checkout line. Any six women will work in this exercise. Pick the last six women you passed while walking down the street. Realize that at least one of those women will be sexually assaulted in a manner that meets the legal definition of rape. Realize that in their lives, all six will experience sexual intrusions routine enough that the women couldn't list them all. Realize that virtually all the men in their lives were trained to see these women as targets, even if all men don't act on that training. This is all normal in the contemporary United States, as well as many other parts of the world. Not 'good' normal nor 'inevitable' normal, but the norm in a society structured on institutionalized male dominance that eroticizes patriarchy's domination/subordination dynamic.

So far, this discussion has gone forward in the context of men's violence against women, sometimes in the context of heterosexual relationships, but rape happens in many other ways. Men can rape lesbians as well as straight women, of course. Men also are violent against other men, and some of that violence is sexual; men sometimes rape other men. A feminist analysis of men's sexual violence against women is crucial to understanding men's sexual violence, no matter who is the victim. Once the domination/subordination dynamic between men and women is eroticized in patriarchy, then all sexual activity becomes defined as a potential site of domination, which can be mapped onto any encounter.

Rape Culture

First used in the 1970s, the term 'rape culture' was in wide circulation by the 1990s,[100] not only within feminism but even in mainstream media. Contrarians who doubted the extent of sexual violence in patriarchy, especially on college campuses, were prominently featured in mainstream media,[101] but a growing body of research documented the reality of women's experiences of men's violence.[102]

So, many feminists were surprised when in 2014 a debate erupted within the anti-violence movement about the appropriate boundaries of the discussion about rape and rape culture, sparked by a statement from one of the largest and most influential groups, the Rape, Abuse and Incest National Network. In a document about sexual assault on college campuses, RAINN stated:

> In the last few years, there has been an unfortunate trend towards blaming 'rape culture' for the extensive problem of sexual violence on campuses. While it is helpful to point out the systemic barriers to addressing the problem, it is important to not lose sight of a simple fact: Rape is caused not by cultural factors but by the conscious decisions, of a small percentage of the community, to commit a violent crime.[103]

---

100 One key collection of essays, first published in 1993, was Emilie Buchwald, Pamela Fletcher, and Martha Roth, eds., *Transforming a Rape Culture* (Minneapolis, MN: Milkweed Editions, 2005, 2nd edition).

101 A prominent early voice was Katie Roiphe, whose book downplayed the 'rape crisis' and was embraced in mainstream culture but sharply critiqued within feminism. *The Morning After: Fear, Sex and Feminism* (New York: Little, Brown and Co., 1993).

102 The first issue of the scholarly journal *Violence Against Women*, edited by sociologist Claire Renzetti, was published in 1995, signaling the importance of research on the issue.

103 Letter from Rape, Abuse and Incest National Network to White House Task Force to Protect Students from Sexual Assault, February 28, 2014. <http://rainn.

Conservative commentators celebrated the statement, using it to condemn the always-demonizable feminists for their allegedly unfair treatment of men and allegedly crazy critique of masculinity,[104] while feminist bloggers vigorously defended the importance of understanding rape culture.[105] The mass media's attention waned quickly, but the dust-up leaves two important questions:

Question #1: Do we live in a rape culture, or is rape (as it is legally defined) perpetrated by a relatively small number of predatory men?

Question #2: Is rape a clearly definable crime, or are there gray areas in sexual encounters that defy easy categorization as either consensual or non-consensual?

The answer to both questions is, of course, yes. In both questions, both assertions are true in some sense. With both questions, a feminist analysis of patriarchy helps clarify.

Question #1: Individual men rape in a rape culture

Because no human activity takes place in an ideological vacuum—the ideas in our heads affect the way we behave—it's hard to make sense of the amount of sexual violence without the concepts of patriarchy and rape culture. A rape culture doesn't command men to rape but does blur the line between consensual sex and non-consensual rape, and also reduces the likelihood that rapists will be identified, arrested, prosecuted, convicted, and punished. It's hard to imagine meaningful

---

org/images/03-2014/WH-Task-Force-RAINN-Recommendations.pdf>

104 Caroline Kitchens, "It's Time to End 'Rape Culture' Hysteria," *Time* Magazine, March 20, 2014. <http://time.com/30545/its-time-to-end-rape-culture-hysteria/>

105 Amanda Marcotte, "RAINN Denounces, Doesn't Understand the Concept of 'Rape Culture,'" *Slate*, March 18, 2014. <http://www.slate.com/blogs/xx_factor/2014/03/18/rainn_attacks_the_phrase_rape_culture_in_its_recommendations_to_the_white.html>

efforts to reduce, and someday eliminate, rape without talking openly and honestly about the cultural context in which individuals act.

That's why the "simple fact" RAINN asserts in that paragraph—"Rape is caused not by cultural factors but by the conscious decisions, of a small percentage of the community, to commit a violent crime"—is hardly simple. First, the language is confusing. Rape is perpetrated by a small percentage of men, but rape is caused by many factors, individual and cultural. That confusion gives way to what seems like deliberate obfuscation in the next paragraph:

> This has led to an inclination to focus on particular segments of the student population (e.g., athletes), particular aspects of campus culture (e.g., the Greek system), or traits that are common in many millions of law-abiding Americans (e.g., 'masculinity'), rather than on the subpopulation at fault: those who choose to commit rape. This trend has the paradoxical effect of making it harder to stop sexual violence, since it removes the focus from the individual at fault, and seemingly mitigates personal responsibility for his or her own actions.

Why this reluctance to discuss the consequences of patriarchy's sex/gender norms? Why should we fear talking about the socialization process by which boys and men, law-abiding or otherwise, are trained to see themselves as naturally dominant over women and to see women as sexual objects? Why should we fear asking critical questions about all-male spaces, such as athletic teams and fraternities, where these patriarchal attitudes might be intensely reinforced? That does not mean all men are rapists, that all male athletes are rapists, or that all fraternity members are rapists. All it means is that if we want to stop sexual violence, we should think about how men are socialized in patriarchy.

Although we shouldn't be afraid of a feminist analysis, looking honestly at how men are socialized is not easy. Here's an example: As part of a pledge event, Yale University fraternity members marched on campus shouting sexist chants, including "No means yes, yes means anal."[106] The reference to the anti-rape message "No means no" mocks women's demand that men listen to them and rejects the idea that women can refuse men's demand for sex. "Yes means anal"—that is, women who agree to sex are implicitly agreeing to anything a man wants, including anal penetration—asserts that men's pleasure always should be central.

In this one chant, these men of Yale—one of the most elite universities in the United States, which has produced some of the country's most powerful business and political leaders, including five presidents—clearly express a patriarchal view of sex/gender. Their chant is an endorsement of rape and a celebration of rape culture.

Question #2: Sexual coercion and consent

Consider a hypothetical: A young man and woman are on a first date. The man decides early in the evening that he would like to have sexual intercourse and in conversation makes clear his attraction to her. He does not intend to force her to have sex, but he is assertive in a way that she interprets to mean that he 'won't take no for an answer'. The woman does not want to have sex, but she is uncertain of how he will react if she rejects his advance. Alone in his dorm room—in a setting

---

106 Sam Greenberg, "DKE chants on Old Campus spark controversy," *Yale Daily News*, October 14, 2010. <http://yaledailynews.com/crosscampus/2010/10/14/dke-chants-on-old-campus-spark-controversy/>; and Diane L. Rosenfeld, "Who Are You Calling a 'Ho'?: Challenging the Porn Culture on Campus," in Melinda Tankard Reist and Abigail Bray, eds., *Big Porn Inc: Exposing the Harms of the Global Pornography Industry* (North Melbourne, Australia: Spinifex Press, 2011), p. 41.

in which his physical strength means she likely could not prevent him from raping her—she offers to perform oral sex, hoping that will satisfy him and allow her to get home without a confrontation that could become too intense, even violent. She does not tell him what she is thinking, out of fear of how he may react. The man accepts the offer of oral sex, and the evening ends without conflict.

If that sexual activity happened—and it does happen, it's an experience that women have described[107]—should we label the encounter as consensual sex or rape? In legal terms, this clearly is not rape. So, it's consensual sex. No problem, right?

Consider some other potentially relevant factors: If a year before that situation, the woman had been raped while on a date, would that change our assessment? If she had been sexually assaulted as a child and still, years later, goes into survival mode when feeling a sexualized threat present? If this were a college campus and the man was a well-known athlete, and she feared the system would ignore her complaint to protect him? By legal standards, this still is not rape. But by human standards, does this feel like fully consensual sex?

Critics often accused second-wave radical feminists such as Andrea Dworkin and Catharine MacKinnon of claiming that all heterosexual sex is rape, which their critics deride as a self-evidently absurd claim, which is meant to prove that perhaps not only those writers but all of radical feminism is absurd. But such caricatures avoid the difficult question these feminists raised: In women's experience, how much consensual sex is consented to but not wanted? How much consensual sex is consented to out of fear? Out of insecurity? How much

---

107 Lynn Phillips, *Flirting with Danger: Young Women's Reflections on Sexuality and Domination* (New York: New York University Press, 2000); and Sut Jhally and Andrew Killoy, dir., "Flirting with Danger: Power and Choice in Heterosexual Relationships" (Northampton, MA: Media Education Foundation, 2012).

consensual sex is consented to simply because the woman finds it easier to have sex than to try to communicate with the man about her emotional state at the moment?

Not all heterosexual sex in patriarchy is rape. But once we get past that statement, do we dare ask about the range of women's experience of heterosexual sex in patriarchy?

To complicate things further, we must ask not only what acts constitute rape, but from whose perspective do we evaluate these acts? In one study of sexual assault on college campuses, only 27% of women whose experience met the legal definition of rape labeled themselves as rape victims; 47% of the men who had raped said they expected to engage in a similar assault in the future; and 88% of men who reported an assault that met the legal definition of rape were adamant that they had not raped.[108] We live in a culture in which the sex/domination nexus is so tight that victim and victimizer alike often do not recognize the violence in actions that society has deemed violent enough to be illegal. It seems fair to describe such a society as a rape culture.

With an intersectional framework in mind—in a rape culture where race and class privilege operate along with patriarchy—it's possible to analyze the social/political forces that could lead a judge to sentence a man convicted of sexual assault to a slap-on-the-wrist six-month jail sentence, because the judge determined, "A prison sentence would have a severe impact on him. I think he will not be a danger to others."[109]

---

108 From the Ms. Magazine Project on Campus Sexual Assault, summarized in Mary P. Koss, "Hidden Rape: Sexual Aggression and Victimization in a National Sample of Students in Higher Education," in Ann Wolbert Burgess, ed., *Rape and Sexual Assault II* (New York: Garland, 1988), pp. 3–25.

109 Liam Stack, "Light Sentence for Brock Turner in Stanford Rape Case Draws Outrage," *New York Times*, June 6, 2016. <http://www.nytimes.com/2016/06/07/us/outrage-in-stanford-rape-case-over-dueling-statements-of-victim-and-attackers-father.html?_r=0>

The man, a white Stanford University student and champion swimmer, was convicted in a jury trial that produced unambiguous evidence of the assault (technically, because the man had not yet penetrated the woman with his penis and only his fingers—two other students happened by the scene and stopped the man from continuing the assault—the rapist wasn't convicted of rape, but other sexual assault charges).

Even more illustrative of the devaluation of women was the character-reference letter to the judge from a female friend of the man, who said she knew that her childhood friend was being unfairly maligned, because "rape on campuses isn't always because people are rapists." The good guys—the rapists who aren't rapists, such as her friend, the man convicted of three felony counts of sexual assault—certainly do make mistakes, when they drink too much. Her letter explained:

> This is completely different from a woman getting kidnapped and raped as she is walking to her car in a parking lot. That is a rapist. These are not rapists. These are idiot boys and girls having too much to drink and not being aware of their surroundings and having clouded judgement.[110]

It would be easy to attack this woman's lack of concern for the victim, as a failure of feminist solidarity. But let's save our anger for the man's father and his letter to the judge, an archetypal statement of patriarchal solidarity in which he suggested that jail was "a steep price to pay for 20 minutes of action" and pointed out that his son had already suffered by, among other things, losing interest in food (such as "a big ribeye steak to grill" or "his favorite snack"). The source of the problems on

---

110 Gabriella Paiella, "Brock Turner's Childhood Friend Blames His Felony Sexual-Assault Conviction on Political Correctness," *New York Magazine*, June 6, 2016. <http://nymag.com/thecut/2016/06/brock-turners-friend-pens-letter-of-support.html>

college campuses, according to the father's analysis: "alcohol consumption and sexual promiscuity."[111]

I do not offer this example from a position of smug superiority. Once again: I was socialized as a man in patriarchy. I am confident that I have never engaged in a sexual act that meets the legal definition of rape, but I am not confident that in every sexual experience with a woman she consented to everything in the fullest sense. That's not a covert way of hinting that my sexual history is full of dramatic moments, but instead a recognition of the complexity of these interactions. I'm confident that as I matured, I was clearer about these dynamics and better able to communicate with a partner, but even in healthy relationships such communication can get short-circuited. I don't like having to think about this, but I understand it would be dangerous not to think about it.

Rape's Reality

Whatever disagreements about the role of patriarchal culture in men's violence, there are clear patterns in how women adapt their behavior to live in such a culture. An easy way to illustrate that is an exercise that anti-violence educators have developed to make the reality of rape visible to men.

In an audience with men and women, the facilitator poses a simple question, directed first to the men only: "What actions have you taken in the past week to minimize your risk of being sexually assaulted?" The men in the room usually look puzzled, because they can't think of any such actions. When

---

111 Elle Hunt, "'20 minutes of action': father defends Stanford student son convicted of sexual assault," *The Guardian*, June 5, 2016. <http://www.theguardian.com/us-news/2016/jun/06/father-stanford-university-student-brock-turner-sexual-assault-statement>

I have used this exercise, most often a man will finally say, "Well, I tried to make sure I didn't go to prison," which elicits giggling, though prison rape is of course not a joke, nor is the fact that men outside of prison sometimes rape other men. After a moment of silence, most people in the room can see where the exercise is heading.

When the same question is posed to the women, they start shouting out their many strategies, which include careful attention to where they are, at what time of day/night, with whom. Women talk about reducing the likelihood they will be in a place where a stranger could surprise them and take control without being seen. Women also talk about how they minimize the risks around men they know socially, such as at parties and bars, especially involving alcohol and the fear of being drugged. Women talk about the care they take when going on a date, such as alerting a friend that they are going out with a man for the first time and making sure the friend's phone will be on in case of a call for help. And then there are the strategies around weapons—everything from pocket knives to pepper spray to car keys held tightly between the fingers to increase the debilitating effect of a quick jab.

Women also talk a lot about decisions they make about clothing, one of the subjects that demonstrates how difficult it can be to juggle the expectations of men and the threat men pose. Going to a party or bar, heterosexual women who want to be accepted in a social network often strive to look attractive, which creates pressure to display their bodies in tight and revealing clothes. At the same time, the fear of rape can suggest a strategy of hiding their bodies in loose-fitting clothes. Different women make different decisions, but what's most important in this exercise is for men to realize how present the threat of rape is in women's lives and how many decisions they make about that threat. As Gail Dines puts it, when a young woman goes out, the culture is teaching her that "the only alternative to looking fuckable is to be invisible."[112]

That exercise also often leads into a broader discussion, not just of rape but the routine behavior of men that isn't rape but feels invasive, the reality of sexual intrusion. At one university where I used the exercise, a woman explained that in addition to all she does to try to avoid being raped, the way men sometimes behave in everyday life can feel like an assault. "I like to dance but have pretty much stopped going to clubs," she said. "I just got tired of men I didn't know coming up to me on the dance floor and grinding on me." I asked the women in the room, "Does that happen? Do men do that uninvited?" Many of the women nodded. As I asked the question, I paid attention to the faces of the men in the room, some of whom quickly looked at the floor. They knew what the women meant, because they had engaged in that grinding themselves, or at least witnessed that behavior by other men. Some of those men enjoyed it, while some enjoyed watching other men do it, and at that moment they realized the price of their pleasure for women.

To be clear: This doesn't mean that all men are rapists, that all sex is rape, or that intimate relationships can never be egalitarian. It does mean, however, that rape is about power *and* sex, about the way men are trained to understand ourselves and to see women. The majority of men do not rape. But consider these other categories:

- Men who do not rape but would be willing to rape if they were sure they would not be punished.
- Men who do not rape but will not intervene when another man rapes.

---

112 Gail Dines, *Pornland: How Porn Hijacked Our Sexuality* (Boston: Beacon, 2010; North Melbourne, Australia: Spinifex Press, 2010), p. 105.

- Men who do not rape but buy sex with women who have been, or likely will be, raped in the context of being prostituted.
- Men who do not rape but are sexually stimulated by films with women in situations that depict rape or rape-like acts.
- Men who do not rape but find the idea of rape sexually arousing.
- Men who do not rape but whose sexual arousal depends on feeling dominant and having power over a woman.

Perhaps I don't need to repeat myself, but just in case I haven't been clear: These men are not rapists. But should we take comfort in the fact that the men in these categories are not, in legal terms, guilty of rape? Are we advancing the cause of ending men's violence against women by focusing only on the acts legally defined as rape?

We have to let go of a comforting illusion—that there is some bright line between men who rape and men who don't rape, between the bad guys and the good guys. That doesn't mean all guys are bad, or that we can't distinguish between levels of bad behavior. It means that if we want to end men's violence against women we have to acknowledge the effect of patriarchal socialization, and such critical self-reflection is rarely a pleasant task, individually or collectively.

Could it be that denying that we live in a rape culture masks a deep-seated fear of that task? If the problem of sexual assault is so deeply entwined with our culture's taken-for-granted assumptions about gender and sexuality, then any serious response to the problem of rape requires us to all get more radical, to take radical feminism seriously. Is that what people are afraid of?

If we decide not to talk about patriarchy because it's too challenging, then let's stop pretending we are going to stop sexual violence and recognize that, at best, all we can do is manage the problem. If we can't talk about patriarchy, then let's admit that we are giving up on the goal of a world without rape.

And let's not forget what that would mean. Let's not forget what rape says about gender, sexuality, and power. In Andrea Dworkin's words:

> Rape signifies that the individual victim and all women have no dignity, no power, no individuality, no real safety. Rape signifies that the individual victim and all women are interchangeable, 'all the same in the dark'. Rape signifies that any woman, no matter how uppity she has become, can be reduced by force or intimidation to the lowest common denominator—a free piece of ass, there for the taking.[113]

---

113 Andrea Dworkin, *Letters from a War Zone* (Brooklyn, NY: Lawrence Hill Books, 1993), p. 119.

PROSTITUTION AND PORNOGRAPHY: 'SEX WORK' OR SEXUAL EXPLOITATION?

The discussion of rape assumes that women are fully human with the same claim to dignity as men and that forcing a woman to have sex against her will is always a violation of that dignity claim. Although in practice some men do not act in accordance with those principles, they are endorsed by virtually everyone in the dominant culture. Within feminism, no matter what the differing intellectual or political perspectives, the agreement would be unanimous.

No such consensus—in the dominant culture or within feminism—exists when the discussion turns to prostitution and pornography, along with the activities in strip bars, commercial phone-sex operations, and massage parlors.

The disagreements begin with decisions about how to name activities that involve the buying and selling of women's bodies for sex. Reflecting a radical feminist perspective, I refer to them as 'the sexual-exploitation industries', while liberal and postmodern feminists typically prefer the term 'sex work'.[114]

These choices signal dramatically different analyses. We can understand these practices as a key part of a patriarchal system in which men attempt to control women and their sexuality, which therefore must be challenged; or as merely a type of labor that women can engage in to their potential advantage, which therefore should be treated as any other form of work.

Once again, my goal is not to map exhaustively these debates within feminism but rather to articulate what I believe to be the political and moral positions consistent with the critique of patriarchy that I find most compelling. This chapter focuses on two questions that capture key elements of the dispute, one about the nature of the system, focused on prostitution, and the other about individual actions within the system, focused on pornography, concluding with reflections about a sexual ethic.

'Sex Work': Justice and Dignity

We seek to build a just society, and in this book I am focused especially on a sex/gender system that could guarantee the dignity of men and women. Because a just society that guarantees dignity for women is impossible in patriarchy— whether the conservative or liberal version of institutionalized

---

114 Carol Leigh, "Inventing Sex Work," in Jill Nagle, ed., *Whores and Other Feminists* (New York: Routledge, 1997), pp. 223–231.

male dominance, the hostile or benevolent version of sexism—we work not only to dismantle the structures of patriarchy but also to imagine what a society beyond patriarchy would look like. One way to clarify our thinking about any particular idea, project, or policy is to ask how it would contribute to human flourishing in a world beyond patriarchy. Hence, here is a simple question about the concept of sex work:

Is it possible to imagine any society achieving a meaningful level of justice if people from one sex/gender class could be routinely bought and sold for sexual services by people from another sex/gender class? If one class of people were defined as 'available to be bought and sold for sexual services', is there any way that class of people would not be assigned subordinate status to the dominant class that does the buying? Is justice possible when the most intimate spaces of the bodies of people in one group can be purchased by people in another group?

Same question, stated differently: If we lived in an egalitarian society with sex/gender justice, would the idea of buying and selling people for sexual services likely emerge at all? If we lived in a society that put the dignity of all people at the center of its mission, would anyone imagine 'sex work'?

Another formulation: You are constructing a society from scratch, with the power not only to write laws (if you decide there should be formal laws) but also to write the stories people tell about themselves, each other, and the larger living world. Would you write stories about how one sex/gender class routinely buys and sells another sex/gender class for sexual pleasure?

Last question: You are speaking with a girl who is considering future vocations. You want her to live in a world with sex/gender justice. She asks you, "What do you think I should be when I grow up?" Do you include 'prostitute' on the list? If she includes that on her list, do you respond in the same way as to other possibilities?

If the answer to these questions is no, perhaps it is because, as Kathleen Barry puts it bluntly, "When the human being is reduced to a body, objectified to sexually service another, whether or not there is consent, violation of the human being has taken place."[115]

This inquiry is about the nature of a system and the predictable consequences of the status and power relations among members of different groups within the system. This inquiry is not a judgment about how any individual makes decisions within the existing patriarchal system, but an exercise in imagining the shape of a non-patriarchal system. Such radical analysis does not ignore individuals and their decisions but starts with the system within which they live.

This presentation of the issue makes it clear that I believe the institution of sex work is incompatible with a just society that fosters human dignity. When I have stated this in public talks and writings, I have been told that this political position is based on moral judgments about sexuality, and I agree. My sex/gender politics has moral underpinnings, just as do the sex/gender politics of those who defend other positions. At the core of my rejection of the idea of sex work are judgments about the appropriate role of sexual behavior in human societies, just as defenses of sex work are based on different judgments about that subject. All these ideas are based on notions of what it means to be human and to live a good life—in other words, moral judgments. No one in the discussion gets to claim they are not making such judgments, though people routinely assert

---

115 Kathleen Barry, *The Prostitution of Sexuality* (New York: New York University Press, 1995), p. 23.

that position. In a healthy conversation, people articulate and defend their moral judgments.

My core moral claim is that sexual behavior plays an important role in creating and maintaining healthy, creative intimacy between people. Sexual interaction, which is central to reproduction and also is pleasurable, should be understood as more than simply our method of reproduction or an act to experience pleasure. We should be careful about imposing rigid rules on sexual behavior, but we should not let a fear of potentially repressive constraints on sexual behavior shut down an important conversation about an unavoidable question, "What is sex for?" I'll return to that at the end of this chapter, but for now want to point out that the typical conservative/religious answer to that (sex is appropriate only in heterosexual marriage) and the typical liberal/secular answer (sex is for whatever a person decides) are both patriarchal answers, flip sides of the same patriarchal coin. The conservative answer gives specific men (husbands and fathers) control of women's sexuality, while the liberal answer makes women's sexuality as widely available to as many men as possible.

A friend captured that reality during the U.S. invasion of Afghanistan in 2001, when U.S. politicians claimed that one goal of the war was to liberate the women and girls of the country from the domination of Afghan men: In this world, women can be either feudal property (in places like Afghanistan) or a capitalist commodity (in places like the United States). In either case, conservative or liberal, patriarchy defines women's sexuality as the thing that men take, with differing opinions as to the conditions under which it can be taken.

The reference to capitalism triggers another common claim, this one from defenders of sex work who acknowledge the harsh conditions under which women routinely work in prostitution. There are many jobs in capitalism—perhaps most jobs—in which people are alienated from self and others because they have lost control over their work and become a tool of capitalist production. So what is the difference between working a job on a factory assembly line and sex work?

I am anti-capitalist and believe that human freedom and capitalism—as that system really exists in the world, not the fantasy version in economics textbooks—are incompatible. I agree that work in capitalism is profoundly alienating. But is there really no difference between renting yourself to an employer who pays you to use your mind and body to produce products and services, and renting yourself to another person who pays you to penetrate your body to achieve sexual pleasure? Lori Watson argues that the claim that selling sex is work just like any other form of work is indefensible on the surface because "if we apply the regulations currently applied to other forms of work to the selling and buying of sex, the acts intrinsic to the 'job' can't be permitted; they are simply inconsistent with regulations governing worker safety, sexual harassment laws, and civil rights."[116]

Of course there are similarities between prostitution and other kinds of work in capitalism. In lots of jobs, the people paying workers are motivated by self-interest in a fashion that may lead them to disregard workers' humanity, and some non-sex-work jobs expose workers to infections/toxins and result in the workplace injuries, which are routine in prostitution and pornography. But the psychological and physical risks are distinctive in sex work. In one study of 130 street prostitutes, 68% met the diagnostic criteria for post-

---

116 Lori Watson, "Why Sex Work Isn't Work," *Logos*, 13:3–4 (2014). <http://logosjournal.com/2014/watson/>; see also Mary Sullivan, *Making Sex Work: A Failed Experiment with Legalising Prostitution* (North Melbourne, Australia: Spinifex Press, 2007).

traumatic stress disorder.[117] Along with the threat of violence from men buying sex, pimps often use coercion and violence to keep women working as prostitutes, leading one team that reviewed research from nine countries to describe prostitution as "multitraumatic."[118]

For the sake of argument, let's assume that policies could be magically devised to protect women in prostitution from violence and ensure a safer work environment, what is generally referred to as 'harm reduction'. In such a setting, would sex work be any different from other forms of work? For me, sexuality is a realm of human experience in which the way we use our bodies is distinctly different from other activities. Sexuality is primarily a vehicle for intimate connection to another human being, an interaction in which we make ourselves vulnerable in ways that are rare in everyday life, a practice through which we explore ourselves with another person. All of those things can happen in other forms of human interaction, but they happen in a distinctive way in sexual behavior. This claim comes not from Hollywood movies' shallow notions of romantic love but out of my experience, and is consistent with the experience of many others. There is considerable variation in the human species, of course, and methods of intimate exploration vary, but the idea that sexuality is a distinctive realm of human experience is widely held.

Before debating sex work, we all should articulate the moral judgments we make about sexuality, reflecting our ideas about what it means to be human and to live a good life. To claim, as I just did, that sexuality is best understood as a vehicle for

---

117 Melissa Farley and Howard Barkan, "Prostitution, Violence, and Post-Traumatic Stress Disorder," *Women & Health*, 27:3 (1998): 37–49.

118 Melissa Farley, et al., "Prostitution and Trafficking in 9 Countries: Update on Violence and Posttraumatic Stress Disorder," *Journal of Trauma Practice*, 2:3/4 (2003): 33–74.

human connection rather than merely for reproduction or pleasure, is indeed a value judgment, just as is any competing claim. If there are no biological 'facts' that clearly establish criteria for evaluating these claims—that is, if we are in the realm of moral philosophy, psychology, and sociology, not science—then I would suggest the key question is: "Which judgments are most consistent with helping people create and maintain stable, decent human communities that can remain in a sustainable relationship with the larger living world?"

Conservatives tend to want to impose narrow answers to shore up patriarchy, while liberals tend to suggest that individuals should be free to act as they wish without considering patriarchy's role in shaping attitudes and behavior. Capitulating to conservatives' repressive norms or embracing liberalism's illusory claim to liberation both take us down dead-end patriarchal paths. I'll return at the end of this chapter to the progressive possibilities, but for now let's remember what sex work in patriarchy is.

Rather than seeing men's control and use of women for sex as natural and stemming from a biological imperative, political scientist Sheila Jeffreys argues that first must exist "the idea of prostitution," the notion that men can buy women's sexuality in various forms, socially constructed out of men's dominance and women's subordination: "The idea of prostitution has to exist in a man's head first if he is to consider using a woman that way. A necessary component of this idea is that it will be sexually exciting to so use a woman."[119] And Kathleen Barry points out that

> the construction of sexuality that reduces sex to a thing and woman to an object is a *public* condition which affects private

---

119 Sheila Jeffreys, *The Idea of Prostitution* (North Melbourne, Australia: Spinifex Press, 1997), p. 3.

> life but has a public reality of its own. The public construction of sex as a social fact of male power sexualizes women as a public fact. The fullest patriarchal reduction of woman to sexed body is prostitution.[120]

Prostitution is an idea about the subordinate status of women in patriarchy, made real in the world through a practice that enacts that subordination. The harm comes in both the idea and the practice. Advocates for normalizing sex work seek to treat prostitution as routine work so that women can take greater control over the conditions of their work to increase their compensation and guarantee their health and safety. Attempts to change the practice of prostitution to improve the lives of women can be well-intentioned, but the effects will be, at best, extremely limited because such reforms do not challenge the idea of prostitution. As long as men believe it is sexually exciting to use a woman, prostitution will be dangerous for women in the short term and will shore up patriarchy in the long term. The patriarchal reduction of a woman to the status of an object that can be used sexually by men is, and always will be, at odds with women's claim to the dignity that comes with fully human status.

Rachel Moran, a woman who rejects the term sex worker to describe her years of surviving prostitution, writes of the inevitable loss of humanity for women: "In prostitution, men dehumanize women and women dehumanize themselves in order to be able to perform the acts men require of them."[121] Cherie Jimenez, who worked off and on for twenty years in prostitution and now runs an exit program in Boston, agrees:

---

120 Barry, *The Prostitution of Sexuality*, p. 22.
121 Rachel Moran, *Paid for: My Journey through Prostitution* (New York: W.W. Norton and Co., 2015: North Melbourne, Australia: Spinifex Press, 2013), p. 181.

"[T]o use your body, to sell your body—it does something to you. Not very many people come out of it whole and in a very healthy way. Even under the best circumstances."[122]

'Sex Workers': Women's Decisions

Just as contentious as the debate within feminism about the nature of sex work is the debate about how to understand the experience of sex workers. Again, language gives away fundamental differences. The term 'sex workers' suggests that working in prostitution and pornography is like any other job. Radical feminists use terms such as 'prostituted women', or 'women used in prostitution', or 'women used in the production of pornography'. Central to the choice of terms is how to understand the nature of the decisions women make. Here I will focus on pornography, graphic sexually explicit material that allows men to continue to use a woman sexually after the sexual act being filmed is over.

First, whatever the terms used, radical feminists who oppose the sexual-exploitation industries do not insult or devalue the women in those industries. Opposition to systems in which men use women is not an attack on those women, which is why many former and current women in the sexual-exploitation industries share the feminist critique of the system.[123] Yet, in recent years radical feminists have been

---

122 Mac McClelland, "Is Prostitution Just another Job?" *New York Magazine*, March 21, 2016. <http://nymag.com/thecut/2016/03/sex-workers-legalization-c-v-r.html>

123 Rebecca Whisnant and Christine Stark, eds., *Not For Sale: Feminists Resisting Prostitution and Pornography* (North Melbourne, Australia: Spinifex Press, 2004); Caroline Norma and Melinda Tankard Reist, eds., *Prostitution Narratives: Stories of Survival in the Sex Trade* (North Melbourne, Australia: Spinifex Press, 2016).

tagged with the acronym SWERF (Sex Worker Exclusionary Radical Feminist):

> A person who espouses to be a feminist but who does not believe that women engaged in ANY form of voluntary sex work should be included in the fight for equality, especially in employment or salary parity. This rabid exclusion of an entire class of women is usually a belief based on misplaced uptight morality.[124]

This definition highlights the misunderstanding: Radical feminists do not exclude any women from the fight for equality but rather offer a vision for achieving equality that is different from a liberal/postmodern program that accepts or celebrates the idea of prostitution. There is no exclusion, rabid or more temperate, in a critique of the sexual-exploitation industries, but instead a competing framework for analysis. I believe people have the right to name themselves, and if a woman in the sexual-exploitation industries preferred to be called a sex worker rather than a prostituted woman, for example, I would do so. But respect for a person's preference in self-naming does not require that we abandon an analysis of the larger industries or the patriarchal forces at their core.

In other movements that focus on harmful industrial practices, such as the critique of sweatshop conditions in garment factories in the developing world, no one suggests that the critique is really an attack on the factories' employees who decide to work there. Anti-sweatshop campaigns are not accused of denying the fact that workers have a capacity to make decisions, but rather are understood to be focused on the conditions created by those with more power—in that case, factory owners and managers, and the multinational corporations for which they typically are manufacturing apparel.

---

124 Urban Dictionary. <http://www.urbandictionary.com/define.php?term=Swerf>

So, meaningful discussion of the decisions that individuals make requires attention to the conditions under which people select jobs, which means considering (1) not only the conditions at the moment the decision is made, but the conditions in their lives leading up to that moment, and (2) not just an account of the options available to them that are visible to an outside observer, but their subjective understanding of those options.

Let's consider two aspects of the sexual-exploitation industries that are established by research: The women in these industries have higher levels of childhood sexual assault and lower socio-economic status and education levels compared with the general population.[125] Do those realities affect women's options? Childhood sexual assault often leads survivors to see their value in the world as the ability to produce pleasure for others. Reduced economic and education opportunities can make alternatives seem implausible. Observing these patterns does not mean every individual's life can be explained in the same way, but the patterns reveal important aspects of the conditions under which people make decisions.

Every decision we make is based on what we perceive as the constraints we face and the opportunities available. Those with wealth, power, and status make choices under fewer constraints with more opportunities—colloquially, it seems appropriate to say that they are making 'free' choices. But people under great constraints with few opportunities also make choices—even if they have limited options and seem less free—and one aspect of respecting the human dignity of others is respecting their right and ability to choose. But our

---

125 For example, Jo-Anne Madeleine Stoltz, et al., "Associations between Childhood Maltreatment and Sex Work in a Cohort of Drug-using Youth," *Social Science and Medicine*, 65:6 (2007): 1214–1221. See also the advocacy group Prostitution Research & Education's archive of relevant research online. <http://prostitutionresearch.com/topic/prostitution/>

collective commitment to human dignity demands that we not turn away from the reality of the world in which we all make decisions, including those harsh realities that affect people without wealth, power, privilege, and status.

At this point in the conversation, it's reasonable to want to hear more from the women involved in the buying and selling of sex. If these decisions involve complex realities, would we not be best informed by hearing directly from those living in that complexity? Yes, but of course there is considerable variation in women's experiences and in their assessments of those experiences. For every women who expresses satifaction with sex work, one can find more women who will analyze the patriarchal domination at the core of her experience in the sexual-exploitation industries, such as Rachel Moran, whose experience as a prostituted woman led her to conclude: "A woman's compliance in prostitution is a response to circumstances beyond her control, and this produces an environment which prohibits even the possibility of true consent. There is a difference between consent and reluctant submission."[126]

Rae Story, who was first prostituted at age eighteen, testified that after an adolescence marked by bullying, homelessness, depression, and self-harm:

> I was not in a position to make this choice freely—if we are to understand the nature of freedom to its fullest extent. And nor were most of the other women I met. I worked across the flimsy class divides in prostitution—working class brothels, middle class escort agencies—and all of the women I met carried with them the same bundles of neurosis, addiction and melancholy. Without exception. Many were desperate to scramble out of destitute circumstances, abusive husbands, redundancy, or the

---

126 Moran, *Paid for*, p. 159.

assumptions of ignobility that society presumes of the poor. Most had some relationship with addictive, impulsive or ostentatious, attention seeking behaviours. Oscillating between self-damage and crying out to be liked, respected and admired, as a remedy for whatever incompleteness they falsely believed of themselves. … One doesn't consent, simply, to prostitution, it is rather an impoverished form of bargaining. However as time moves on, the worth of your chips further degenerate. Your self-esteem erodes, your understanding of yourself becomes confused, as the labour necessitates self-denial and psychological suppression. … I didn't choose to leave prostitution, my body chose for me. In the end, it knew better.[127]

How do we determine which voices are most authentic and truly represent women's experiences? Do we count up the pro and con narratives and declare a winner? As much as we would like clear answers, no research project can provide them, for several reasons.

First, as with virtually all such questions, there are dramatic differences in people's conception of the good life. That leads many to shrug and say, "to each her own," which appears the easiest route but leaves us without much guidance for public policy. Even if there is no single truth about the experience of women in prostitution and pornography, as a society we still have to make decisions about the rules we live by, and those rules will be especially important in shaping the lives of the most vulnerable people in society.

Second, individual women sometimes make what feminists have called a "patriarchal bargain … a decision to accept gender rules that disadvantage women in exchange for whatever power one can wrest from the system … an individual strategy designed to manipulate the system to one's

---

127 Rae Story, "Prostitution Survivor Testimony," *Nordic Model Now!* <https://nordicmodelnow.org/testimonial/rae-story/>

best advantage, but one that leaves the system itself intact."[128] That term was coined in 1988, "to indicate the existence of set rules and scripts regulating gender relations, to which both genders accommodate and acquiesce, yet which may nonetheless be contested, redefined, and renegotiated."[129] At any given moment, is a person's account capitulation or challenge?

The problem of conflicting voices is complicated further by another aspect of human experience: We are not at every moment the best judge of our own experience. Take the example of a young woman with the eating disorder anorexia nervosa, a person who is thin yet feels overweight and develops an intense fear of gaining weight, which can lead to obsessive dieting and severe health problems. At that moment, the woman may insist that she is overweight and must reduce her food intake. An outside observer suggests that she is underweight and needs to eat more. Which person is right? The woman is accurately conveying how she feels about her body, but the vast majority of outside observers would suggest she is wrong about the actual state of her body. Do we accept the woman's account of her physical health as definitive and beyond challenge, and hence celebrate her desire to diet?

I am edging toward the question of false consciousness, a concept that emerged from Marxist analysis of the ideology of capitalism, the process by which the ideas that justify capitalist domination become the 'common sense' of a culture and lead members of the working class to support the very system that constrains their freedom. Polite people tend to

---

128 Lisa Wade, "Serena Williams' Patriarchal Bargain," *Sociological Images*, May 22, 2011. <https://thesocietypages.org/socimages/2011/05/22/women-damned-if-you-do-damned-if-you-dont/>

129 Deniz Kandiyoti, "Bargaining with Patriarchy," *Gender and Society*, 2:3 (1988): 286.

avoid asserting that others have false consciousness because it's rude to tell people that they don't understand themselves and their circumstances. Yet we all know from our own experience that at some points in our lives we didn't understand ourselves very well and that someone else was better able to analyze our behavior. As a result of insights we gain from others, we often change our ideas and behavior. Polite or not, it's clear from our own lives that people—including me, and anyone reading this—often experience false consciousness. If that term is distasteful, pick from others that have been offered—repressive satisfactions, false needs, adaptive preferences.

Marxist critic Herbert Marcuse argued in the 1960s that in capitalism people develop, and pursue the satisfaction of, needs that are contrary to real liberation. These are false needs that we should strive to replace with true needs, "the abandonment of repressive satisfaction."[130] At the end of the decade, he wrote, "A universe of human relationships no longer mediated by the market, no longer based on competitive exploitation or terror, demands a sensitivity freed from the repressive satisfactions of the unfree societies."[131]

According to Sandra Bartky, who identified the "fashion-beauty complex" as a key producer and regulator of ideas about femininity that undermine women's flourishing:

> Repressive satisfaction fastens us to the established order of domination, for the same system which produces false needs also controls the conditions under which such needs can be satisfied. 'False needs', it might be ventured, are needs which are produced through indoctrination, psychological manipulation,

---

130 Herbert Marcuse, *One-Dimensional Man: Studies in the Ideology of Advanced Industrial Society* (New York: Routledge Classics, 2002), p. 9.

131 Herbert Marcuse, *An Essay on Liberation* (Boston: Beacon, 1969), p. 27. <https://www.marxists.org/reference/archive/marcuse/works/1969/essay-liberation.htm>

and the denial of autonomy; they are needs whose possession and satisfaction benefit not the subject who has them but a social order whose interest lies in domination.[132]

Other scholars have examined 'adaptive preference formation', how we alter our preferences, whether consciously or unconsciously, in light of the options available to us. Serene Khader defines adaptive preferences as decisions people make that are "incompatible with an agent's basic wellbeing that formed under unjust conditions—and that an agent would reverse upon exposure to better conditions."[133]

If all that's not complicated enough, add another factor: *People often express support for a system they work in because* at that moment in time it is in their short-term self-interest to do so. Most everyone who has ever had a job with a boss knows that we sometimes say things we don't believe to be true—such as, "I think my boss is a great manager"—to make it possible to continue making a living. Sometimes we convince ourselves that we believe it in order to reduce cognitive dissonance and make it easier to get through the day.

Here's an example of the messiness of all this, one that hits close to home for a university professor—graduate students' role in the academic game. Many graduate students work in teaching assistant positions with low pay and long hours, and they enroll in graduate seminars that are sometimes taught by pompous professors who believe themselves to be a lot smarter than they actually are. Ask the graduate students in any academic department what they think of the system in which they are being trained—and perhaps someday hope

---

132 Sandra Lee Bartky, *Femininity and Domination: Studies in the Phenomenology of Oppression* (New York: Routledge, 1990), p. 42.

133 Serene J. Khader, "Must Theorizing about Adaptive Preferences Deny Women's Agency?" *Journal of Applied Philosophy*, 29:4 (2012): 302.

to work as a professor—and you will get a wide variety of answers. Some will explain that the system exploits graduate students as underpaid labor and that the faculty members routinely inflate the value of their own research to rationalize their privileged status. Others will say they respect their professors and are honored to be part of the team. Some who endorse the system while students will tell quite a different story after they graduate and no longer are beholden to those supervising professors. Others will believe in the integrity of the system throughout their lives.

All of these views exist within a graduate student population that is working and studying in the same department, at the same university, in the same academic system. Whose assessments, at which point in time, should we trust when we consider how to modify the rules for the department? Which voices from a group working under such constraints are 'authentic'?

Men's Choices

The debate about prostitution and pornography typically focuses on women's choices, but it's crucial to shift the focus. While women's decisions to participate in the sexual-exploitation industries are complex, men's choices are fairly simple. Men who buy and sell women's bodies in prostitution and pornography often attempt to avoid uncomfortable questions about why they are buying sexual pleasure by claiming that these women are 'freely choosing' that occupation.

Male pornography users in one study agreed that most of what they watched featured men dominating women, which was not seen as distasteful or deserving of critique but instead "was more likely to be minimized through humor or distancing, or rationalized through claims around individual choice on one hand and biological realities on the other."[134] Here's how one male pornography user put it in an email message to me:

> While reading your article there is one thing that I really wanted to point out to you. It's something I've always wanted to scream at all the feminists out there who hate pornography. *No one makes the girls do it.* They choose to do it. And they get paid to do it. Some of them get paid quite well. In fact, the ones that don't get paid that well are still making a lot of money for the little amount of time it takes to make a porno.

This sums up the standard way in which many men (and some women) derail any call for critical self-reflection about their use of pornography—three assertions, leading to a comfortable conclusion:

> Assertion #1: The women in pornography choose it, and
> Assertion #2: they get paid a lot, and
> Assertion #3: those who don't get paid a lot still have it easy because they are being paid for getting fucked, which is easy.
> Conclusion: Therefore, I need not think about why I opt to attain sexual gratification by using the women in pornography.

For the sake of argument, let's assume the assertions are accurate. Why does that eliminate the need for critical self-reflection on the part of pornography consumers? I believe that men are moral agents and we therefore are obligated to assess the consequences of our actions. We can start, selfishly, on questions about the effect of using pornography on men. When we routinely gain sexual pleasure through viewing women being dominated and degraded sexually (the theme of much, possibly the majority of, pornography), what are we

---

134 Aleksandra Antevska and Nicola Gavey, "'Out of Sight and Out of Mind': Detachment and Men's Consumption of Male Sexual Dominance and Female Submission in Pornography," *Men and Masculinities*, 18:5 (2015): 616.

saying about ourselves? When many women in pornography have testified about how they were hurt in the industry, why do we brush those stories aside?

That kind of critical self-reflection is difficult because it demands that we recognize how we were socialized to eroticize domination, which has implications for how we understand and experience ourselves and our sexual desire, along with the obvious implications for women. The cheap and seemingly easy way to avoid grappling with ourselves and our socialization is to complete the conclusion above with a grim unstated assumption: "I need not think about why I want to attain sexual gratification by using the women in pornography because *that's what women are for, to get fucked*."

When men use women in pornography and prostitution—whether or not we say it out loud, whether or not we even think about the question—we are implicitly endorsing that idea: *That's what women are for, to get fucked.*

When men decide not to participate in the sexual-exploitation industries—either in selling or buying women's sexuality—we are stating that we believe women are fully human, deserving of dignity, and do not exist to satisfy men's sexual pleasure. When we make that choice, men are also stating that we believe we are fully human, too.

Men cannot evade these decisions. Neither can women, though it is easy to understand why many women seek to insulate themselves from these questions. For example, after I had summarized for a group of young women the feminist critique of pornography (which they had never heard of), one of the students (in her early 20s) suggested that older people (such as myself, then in my mid-50s) are out of step with young people, including young women. Yes, some pornography is nasty, she said, but she and her friends don't get all worked up—it's just porn.

I offered a hypothetical to test her assertion: Imagine that heterosexual women in your social network are asked out by two guys. The men are equivalent in all the ways that matter to you—sense of humor, intelligence, appearance—and the only clear difference is that one regularly masturbates to pornography and the other never looks at it. Who would you rather go out with? The student winces and acknowledges that she—and most, if not all, of her friends—would choose the non-porn user.

Why the disparity between the stated commitment to being porn-friendly and the actual preference in partners? Further conversation with those students, and many others, suggests that women know what pornography is (male dominance made sexually arousing) and how men use it (as a masturbation facilitator, which helps condition their sexual imaginations to that dominance), but feel a sense of resignation about contemporary pop culture. Do heterosexual women want partners whose sexual imagination has been shaped by making women's subordination a sexual turn-on? "There's no sense in asking them to stop using it," one woman told me, "because they won't." Perhaps some women profess not to be bothered by pornography when they believe they have no options, and if they have never heard of the feminist critique of pornography they cannot consider how that creates options.

What Is Sex For?

I am confident in making the claims that (1) women are fully human and that the sexual-exploitation industries are inconsistent with human dignity, and (2) however complicated women's options are in patriarchy, we should focus first on men's decisions to participate in the buying and selling of women for sex.

On the question of "what is sex for?" I am more hesitant to make definitive claims. I believe that in a healthy society, sex should not be reduced to reproduction or pleasure-acquisition. But sex can, and does, play a variety of roles in our lives, which can change within one's own lifetime and vary between individuals and cultures. Any answer will be specific to time and place. When we are young, for example, sex might be primarily a way for us to explore ourselves as we develop emotionally. As mature adults, sex might be primarily a way to establish stable bonds with a partner.

At this point in history, in contemporary U.S. culture, I worry about how much of life has become commodified and mass-mediated—about contemporary capitalism's obsession with pulling every aspect of human life into the market, and advanced-technology's colonization of our experiences through screens. Combining those concerns with a critique of patriarchy, I return to the power of sexuality to help us connect in meaningful ways to another person—sexuality as a form of communication, part of the ongoing quest to touch and be touched, to be truly alive. James Baldwin got to the heart of this:

> I think the inability to love is the central problem, because the inability masks a certain terror, and that terror is the terror of being touched. And, if you can't be touched, you can't be changed. And, if you can't be changed, you can't be alive.[135]

To assert that sexuality is centrally about love is not to limit our sexual connections to some notion of divinely sanctioned heterosexual marriage or Hollywood-defined romance.

---

135 James Baldwin, interview in *The Advocate*, excerpted in the *Utne Reader* (July/August 2002), p. 100.

Suggesting that the central role of sexual connection in human society has something to do with love is to open up our exploration, to get over the terror of being touched.

Though love defies easy definition, it's easy to identify the sexual-exploitation industries' answer to "what's love got to do with it?" Nothing.

More than two decades ago, when I first started thinking about this question, I kept coming back to the phrase to describe an argument that is intense but which doesn't really advance our understanding—we say that such a debate "produced more heat than light." Much of the talk about sexuality in contemporary culture is in terms of heat: Is the sex you are having hot?

What if our discussions about sexual activity—our embodied connections to another person—were less about heat and more about light? What if instead of desperately seeking hot sex, we searched for a way to produce light when we touch? What if such touch were about finding a way to create light between people so that we could see ourselves and each other better? If the goal is knowing ourselves and each other like that, then what we need is not really heat but light to illuminate the path. How do we touch and talk to each other to shine that light?

Though there is no sexual instruction manual to tell us how to generate that light, I do not hesitate to suggest that the sexual-exploitation industries leave us in the dark.

TRANSGENDERISM: BIOLOGY, POLITICS, ECOLOGY

On the issue of rape, the tensions within feminism in the United States over the analysis of patriarchy have not posed a serious threat to the unity of the movement to end sexual violence. But the debates around patriarchy and the sexual-exploitation industries—contentious enough to earn the label 'sex wars' in the 1980s—have left feminism fractured, with differences that sometimes appear irreconcilable. Just as contentious, and even more emotionally intense, is the ongoing debate about the ideology of the transgender movement, which once again highlights the differences over the concept of patriarchy between radical and liberal/postmodern feminism.

For many years I avoided writing about this subject, hesitant to join such a highly charged debate.[136] But as the expanding public conversation about the issue continually ignored or

---

136 Michelle Goldberg, "What Is a Woman? The Dispute between Radical Feminism and Transgenderism," *New Yorker*, August 4, 2014. <http://www.newyorker.com/magazine/2014/08/04/woman-2>

marginalized critical feminist and ecological perspectives—
which was made clear to me when a national newsmagazine
ran a cover story on "America's Next Civil Rights Frontier"[137]—
I wrote an essay published online in 2014 in which I attempted
to lay out a clear, step-by-step critique in language that was
as non-inflammatory as possible, though my conclusion
was blunt:

> Transgenderism is a liberal, individualist, medicalized response
> to the problem of patriarchy's rigid, repressive, and reactionary
> gender norms. Radical feminism is a radical, structural,
> politicized response. On the surface, transgenderism may seem
> to be a more revolutionary approach, but radical feminism offers
> a deeper critique of the domination/subordination dynamic at
> the heart of patriarchy and a more promising path to liberation.[138]

I received a number of negative responses to the essay, but
the most intriguing reactions were from people in left/
progressive/feminist politics who told me they agreed with
the analysis I had presented but felt they couldn't express such
an opinion publicly without becoming a target of transgender
activists and allies. A stunted dialogue constrained by such
political/intellectual fear is not healthy for any movement,
and so I abandoned my original plan to write only that one
essay in order to explore more deeply the issue and that fear.[139]

---

137 Katy Steinmetz, "The Transgender Tipping Point: America's Next Civil Rights
     Frontier," *Time*, June 4, 2014, pp. 38–46. The issues' cover photo was of
     transgender actor Laverne Cox of the television show *Orange Is the New Black*.

138 Robert Jensen, "Some basic propositions about sex, gender, and patriarchy,"
     Dissident Voice, June 13, 2014. <http://dissidentvoice.org/2014/06/some-basic-
     propositions-about-sex-gender-and-patriarchy/>

139 Robert Jensen, "There are limits: Ecological and social implications of
     trans and climate change," *Dissident Voice*, September 12, 2014, <http://
     dissidentvoice.org/2014/09/ecological-and-social-implications-of-trans-and-
     climate-change/>; "Feminism unheeded," *Nation of Change*, January 8, 2015.
     <http://www.nationofchange.org/2015/01/08/feminism-unheeded/>; and

The next year, when the Bruce/Caitlyn Jenner story[140] was celebrated in pop culture and the *New York Times* launched an editorial campaign that ignored any critical analysis, feminist or otherwise,[141] it seemed more important than ever to grapple with the ideology at the heart of the transgender movement, which was being asserted but not adequately explained.

A caveat: It can be difficult to distinguish criticism of an ideology or movement from criticism of individuals. This chapter examines the *ideas* on which the transgender movement is based and does not attack people who identify as transgender. I am not contesting transgender people's account of their experience, but rather offering an alternative analysis to understand that experience.

A reminder: As in the previous chapters, I am not presenting myself as a grand arbiter on debates within feminism. Instead I hope to articulate in plain language a framework that raises a number of foundational questions about how we understand ourselves as social and political beings embedded in ecosystems. Although many would like to avoid this issue, transgenderism provides an important window into the fear of confronting patriarchy and the lack of critical thinking about advanced technology, which makes the sometimes tense debate worth our time and energy. This is one of those times that saying "we'll have to agree to disagree" in order to avoid conflict is a lost opportunity for clarifying important questions at the heart of a disagreement.

"A transgender problem for diversity politics," *Dallas Morning News*, June 5, 2015. <http://www.dallasnews.com/opinion/latest-columns/20150605-robert-jensen-a-transgender-problem-for-diversity-politics.ece>

140 Buzz Bissinger, "Call Me Caitlyn," *Vanity Fair*, July 2015, pp. 50–69, 105–106.

141 "Transgender Today," *New York Times*, May 4, 2015. <http://www.nytimes.com/2015/05/04/opinion/the-quest-for-transgender-equality.html>

A Critical Feminist Analysis

A quick summary of the basics that I outlined in the Sex/ Gender and Patriarchy/Feminism chapters, which are central to a discussion of transgenderism:

Male and female humans obviously have different roles in reproduction, what we can call sex-role differentiation. The meaning that societies make of that differentiation is typically called the social construction of gender. In patriarchy, gender-role differentiation supports male power and makes the system's domination/subordination dynamic seem natural and normal; gender in patriarchy is a category that established and reinforces inequality. Patriarchal systems, designed to justify and perpetuate male dominance, are not monolithic or static but adapt to changing conditions and respond to resistance movements. But in general, patriarchy turns biological sex differences into social and political gender inequality.

The gender roles in patriarchy are rigid (men and women are expected to adhere to the assigned norms without deviation), repressive (these norms inhibit the capacity of men and women to develop the full scope of abilities and interests), and reactionary (the gender system strengthens patriarchy's hierarchy). These roles constrain the healthy flourishing of both males and females, but females experience by far the most significant psychological and physical injuries from the system.

The debate within feminism over transgenderism goes back to the 1970s, with a key flash point in 1979 when Janice Raymond published *The Transsexual Empire*.[142] Sheila Jeffreys'

---

142 Janice G. Raymond, *The Transsexual Empire: The Making of the She-Male* (New York: Teachers College Press, 1994, reissued with new introduction).

2014 *Gender Hurts*[143] also was contentious, coming at a time when not only liberal/postmodern feminists embraced transgenderism but some feminists identified with the radical tradition endorsed the transgender movement as well. For example, in repudiating previous statements she had made critical of transgenderism, Gloria Steinem wrote:

> I believe that transgender people, including those who have transitioned, are living out real, authentic lives ... [a]nd what I wrote decades ago does not reflect what we know today as we move away from only the binary boxes of 'masculine' or 'feminine' and begin to live along the full human continuum of identity and expression.[144]

Again, to be clear: I speak for myself, not for a philosophy or a movement, when I suggest Steinem's liberal analysis mischaracterizes "what we know," confuses sex and gender, and incorrectly implies the transgender movement provides a politically productive route to challenging patriarchy. In the remainder of this chapter, I will defend those statements. While some may dismiss any such analysis as "a certain generational grouchiness toward trans people [that] has emerged from a few redoubts of second-wave feminism,"[145] I believe the question, challenge, and concern I raise here require serious engagement, not a flippant dismissal.

---

143 Sheila Jeffreys, *Gender Hurts: A Feminist Analysis of the Politics of Transgenderism* (New York: Routledge, 2014).

144 Gloria Steinem, "On Working Together Over Time," *Advocate*, October 2, 2013. <http://www.advocate.com/commentary/2013/10/02/op-ed-working-together-over-time>

145 Paisley Currah, "General Editor's Introduction," *Transgender Studies Quarterly*, 3:1–2 (2016): 2.

Definitions and Categories

For the sake of clarity and concision, I will use the terms common in the transgender movement, even when I don't agree with the assumptions on which they are based. For example, I use the term 'sex-reassignment surgery' because it is common, though I do not believe that sex categories can be shifted by the procedure; after surgery, a male human's body will in some ways more closely approximate a female body but the person does not become female. Some in the transgender movement now advocate the term "gender-confirming surgery,"[146] which in some ways is even more confusing, if it's meant to imply that the cultural concept of gender can be changed surgically. To conform to the common usage, for example, I will use the term 'transwoman' and the pronouns that an individual prefers when someone born unambiguously male identifies as female/woman, either with or without sex-reassignment surgery.

First, it's important to distinguish intersex conditions from transgenderism. As the major intersex organization puts it:

> People who identify as transgender or transsexual are usually people who are born with typical male or female anatomies but feel as though they've been born into the 'wrong body'. ... People who have intersex conditions have anatomy that is not considered typically male or female. Most people with intersex conditions come to medical attention because doctors or parents notice something unusual about their bodies. In contrast, people who are transgendered have an internal experience of gender identity that is different from most people.[147]

---

146 Leela Ginelle, "Real Talk with Trans People," *Medium*, September 8, 2015. <https://medium.com/matter/real-talk-with-trans-people-57b9aa3b91a8>

147 "What's the Difference between Being Transgender or Transsexual and Having an Intersex Condition?" Intersex Society of North America. <http://www.isna.org/faq/transgender>

Although there is no definitive source on terminology, the National Center for Transgender Equality's definitions are widely used and similar to most others:[148]

> Transgender: A term for people whose gender identity, expression or behavior is different from those typically associated with their assigned sex at birth. Transgender is a broad term and is good for non-transgender people to use. 'Trans' is shorthand for 'transgender'.

> Transsexual: An older term for people whose gender identity is different from their assigned sex at birth who seeks (sic) to transition from male to female or female to male. Many do not prefer this term because it is thought to sound overly clinical.[149]

When talking about the movement and its ideology in general, I will use the terms 'transgender' and 'transgenderism', though some who are part of the movement prefer 'trans' or 'trans*'.

In the American Psychological Association diagnostic manual, the relevant category is "gender dysphoria," which "as a general descriptive term refers to an individual's affective/cognitive discontent with the assigned gender but is more specifically defined when used as a diagnostic category" and "refers to the distress that may accompany the incongruence between one's experienced or expressed gender and one's assigned gender."[150] This term replaced "gender identity disorder" from the previous edition.

Terminology typically is shaped by an understanding of the nature and cause of a condition. Does gender dysphoria

---

148 Another common source is "Transgender Issues," GLAAD Media Reference Guide. <http://www.glaad.org/reference/transgender>

149 "Transgender Terminology," National Center for Transgender Equality. <http://transequality.org/issues/resources/transgender-terminology>

150 *Diagnostic and Statistical Manual of Mental Disorders* (Arlington, VA: American Psychiatric Association, 2013, 5th ed.), p. 451.

reflect a simple variation in the species, or is it a "disorder" as the APA classifies that term: "A mental disorder is a syndrome characterized by clinically significant disturbance in an individual's cognition, emotion regulation, or behavior that reflects a dysfunction in the psychological, biological, or developmental processes underlying mental functioning."[151]

If it is a disorder, is its origin primarily physical or psychological? As one researcher put it, "The etiology of a transgender or transsexual identity remains largely unknown."[152] Although there is speculation about the biological basis for transgenderism, focused primarily on prenatal hormones' effect on brain development, the evidence for "sex atypical cerebral differentiation"[153] is sketchy at best. Moreover, the research seems to ignore the degree to which gender norms are socially constructed and variable across time and place. Not surprisingly, this research rarely includes an acknowledgement, let alone a serious discussion, of patriarchy.[154] In response to the question "Why are some people transgender?," an APA factsheet acknowledges, in slightly less straightforward language, that there is no coherent theory:

> There is no single explanation for why some people are transgender. The diversity of transgender expression and experiences argues against any simple or unitary explanation. Many experts believe that biological factors such as genetic

151 *Ibid.*, p. 20.

152 Walter O. Bockting, "Transgender Identity Development," in Deborah L. Tolman and Lisa M. Diamond, eds., *APA Handbook of Sexuality and Psychology* (Washington, DC: American Psychological Association, 2014), p. 743.

153 Ivanka Savic and Stefan Arver, "Sex Dimorphism of the Brain in Male-to-Female Transsexuals," *Cerebral Cortex*, 21:11 (November 2011): 2525–2533. <http://cercor.oxfordjournals.org/content/21/11/2525>

154 For example, Aruna Saraswat, Jamie D. Weinand, and Joshua D. Safer, "Evidence Supporting the Biologic Nature of Gender Identity," *Endocrine Practice*, 21:2 (2015): 199–204.

influences and prenatal hormone levels, early experiences, and experiences later in adolescence or adulthood may all contribute to the development of transgender identities.[155]

Norman Spack, an endocrinologist at Boston Children's Hospital known for his treatment of transgender children, puts transgenderism in the category of "relatively rare diseases and conditions."[156] Not all in the transgender movement agree with this medicalizing and pathologizing language, but anyone who supports medical treatment as a response to an individual's distress implicitly accepts the label of a disorder, disease, or condition. More recently, Spack referred to it as "a medical condition," saying that "surgical and medical aspects" of care should be covered by insurance. "First you have to not make it a mental illness. You have to define it as a *physical problem* (emphasis added) which it is,"[157] which to him means removing it from the APA manual, as happened with homosexuality.

The grouping together of lesbian/gay and transgender identities is common, seen in the common acronym 'LGBT' and variations, but there are key differences that shouldn't be overlooked. While there are shared concerns about discrimination and threats of violence, lesbians and gay men do not suggest that same-sex attraction is a condition that requires treatment. When lesbians and gay men rejected the label of mental illness, they didn't seek to redefine homosexuality as a "physical problem" or a problem of any kind;

---

155 "Answers to Your Questions About Transgender People, Gender Identity and Gender Expression," American Psychological Association. <http://www.apa. org/topics/lgbt/transgender.aspx>

156 Norman P. Spack, "Foreword," in Stephanie Brill and Rachel Pepper, eds., *The Transgender Child: A Handbook for Families and* Professionals (San Francisco: Cleis Press, 2008), p. xi.

157 Charlie Rose Show, "The Brain Series: Gender Identity," PBS, July 9, 2015. <https://charlierose.com/collections/3/clip/21056>

no treatment is necessary, only an end to discrimination. While not all transgender people seek or advocate medical intervention, the transgender movement seems to embrace that possibility as appropriate for those opting for it. And, most important, heterosexual people—even opponents of gay/lesbian rights—understand what same-sex attraction is; the concept is intelligible, even if a specific heterosexual person doesn't experience that attraction. But many people do not understand the nature of transgender claims; even some who support the movement's policy proposals acknowledge that the concept has not been adequately explained.

Ground Rules for Debate

Everyone making proposals about public policies—the rules under which we live together in society—has an obligation to make a clear argument for a proposal, with evidence and reasoning that is accessible to others. We all have personal experiences that are relevant to our understanding of the world and that inform our policy positions, and bringing those experiences to policy discussions is important. When misunderstandings crop up in policy debates, especially when we have revealed aspects of our own lives to others, we may want to tell a person on the other side, "You just don't get it," out of frustration that we are not being understood. That phrase can be used in two different ways.

If people have presented adequate evidence and sound reasoning to establish a proposition, and I refuse to engage with the argument presented, then they are justified in making the claim that I don't get it, perhaps because I am actively deciding not to get it in order to avoid having to concede the argument. But if people assert that I just don't get it before they have presented an argument, or after they have presented a confusing argument, then they are using my alleged inability to understand as a cover for their own failure to make a coherent argument.

The claim "you don't share this experience that I've had, and therefore you can never understand," may turn out to be the case—we try to empathize with others but there are limits to empathy. There may be experiences that are difficult, perhaps even impossible, to convey in words to others. If that is the case, people's inability to explain their experience doesn't negate the experience, but it does limit their ability to argue for public policies that are based solely on their subjective internal experience. In debates over public policy, people have to be able to understand the basis on which others argue for a policy. That means not only testifying to one's experience but also offering an analysis that others can understand.

In discussing these matters with transgender people or transgender allies, I have often been told I don't get it or that I'm not sensitive enough to transgender people's experiences, but I have yet to be presented with a coherent account of transgenderism. At times, transgender people acknowledge this problem. For example, transwoman Christine McGinn said in an interview with transwoman Jennifer Finney Boylan, "You cannot deny the biology of men and women. But where society gets it wrong is the binary. There are plenty of people in between. It's a mystery, and I think it will always be a mystery." She continued in that vein, saying, "I challenge people to define what is male and what is female," but then complained that "there are a lot of feminists and lesbians that do not get the transgender thing at all."[158] To describe transgenderism

---

158 Quoted in Jennifer Finney Boylan, *Stuck in the Middle with You: A Memoir of Parenting in Three Genders* (New York: Crown, 2013), pp. 225–226.

as a mystery that defies definitions (even though there is a definition of male and female based in reproduction), and then suggest that some people fail to "get the transgender thing" is disingenuous, an attempt to cover up the inability to offer a coherent account.

To be clear: I am not suggesting that anyone has an obligation to make their personal history completely understandable to me; much of human experience is indeed mysterious, and I am not the ultimate arbiter of the validity of anyone's account of their experience. But one cannot demand support for public policy proposals based solely on such claims. And when people making proposals offer claims that appear to be internally contradictory, we all have a right to ask for clarification.

People questioning the transgender ideology are often accused of negating the experience of transgender people and/or being transphobic.[159] But the feminists I consider allies do not suggest that transgender people's experiences in regard to gender norms are not real, but instead offer an alternative way to explore those experiences. To offer a good-faith challenge to another person's interpretation of their experience, political or psychological, does not negate that person. When a factory worker insists that a union would be bad for the workers, labor organizers don't hesitate to challenge that person's interpretation of the relationship between workers, managers, and owners. Such an argument doesn't negate the worker's experience or devalue the worker as a person, but rather says, "Here's another way to look at it." When we challenge the self-perception of people suffering from anorexia nervosa who believe they need to lose weight, we aren't suggesting they

---

159 "Smash the Cistem: A Note on Bob Jensen," MonkeyWrench Books. <https://genderidentitywatch.files.wordpress.com/2014/07/smash-the-cistem_-a-note-on-bob-jensen.pdf>

really don't feel overweight, but rather we are offering another way to analyze that sense they have of themselves.

My feminist politics are rooted in a rejection of patriarchy's rigid, repressive, and reactionary gender norms, and so I'm not sure how 'transphobia' describes my position. If the term is defined as fear or hatred of people who identify as transgender, I can only say that I'm not afraid of, and don't hate, any transgender person I've ever met. If more generally the term suggests antagonism toward people who identify as transgender, I don't believe that presenting an alternative explanation is antagonistic.

It should go without saying—but I will say it anyway—that there is no justification for challenging the dignity of, or allowing discrimination against, transgender people, and that violence against transgender people is unacceptable. The law, and common decency, should protect people, especially those in vulnerable positions.

So, to be clear, I believe transgender people exist. That is, "people whose gender identity, expression or behavior is different from those typically associated with their assigned sex at birth"[160] exist. The debate is about how to best understand that experience. Transgender people, as individuals, can decide whether or not they want to engage in conversation with others about that question—all people have the right to decide how and when they discuss personal matters with others. But when participating in a movement that argues for changes in public policies, transgender people have an obligation to present a coherent account of their position and respond to good-faith challenges.

---

160 "Transgender Terminology," National Center for Transgender Equality. <http://transequality.org/issues/resources/transgender-terminology>

Transgender claims have led to a variety of policy debates, especially concerning the rules for female-only spaces that are designed to foster a sense of safety and expressive freedom for females generally (such as cultural institutions, with one of the most well-known cases being the Michigan Womyn's Music Festival)[161] and particularly to create safety for females who have been victims of male violence (such as rape crisis and domestic violence centers, where transwomen have demanded to be allowed to counsel female rape victims).[162] Public funding for sex-reassignment surgery (such as through Medicare in the U.S., which dropped its exclusion of coverage in 2014) and mandatory insurance coverage for such treatments (laws vary state by state, and the federal Affordable Care Act prohibits denial of coverage based on gender identity)[163] involve serious public health decisions about the concept of 'medically necessary' that cannot be resolved by simplistic freedom-to-choose arguments. Practices involving children that are questionable on public health grounds, such as the use of puberty suppression to interfere with children's

---

161 Trudy Ring, "This Year's Michigan Womyn's Music Festival Will Be the Last," Advocate.com, April, 21 2015. <http://www.advocate.com/michfest/2015/04/21/years-michigan-womyns-music-festival-will-be-last>

162 Vancouver Rape Relief Society v. Nixon et al., British Columbia Supreme Court, 2003. <http://www.rapereliefshelter.bc.ca/learn/resources/chronology-events-kimberly-nixon-vs-vancouver-rape-relief-society>

163 Abby Goodnough and Margot Sanger-Katz, "Health Care Rules Proposed to Shield Transgender Patients from Bias," New York Times, September 3, 2015. <http://www.nytimes.com/2015/09/04/us/health-care-rules-proposed-to-shield-transgender-patients-from-bias.html?_r=1>; and U.S. Department of Health & Human Services, "HHS finalizes rule to improve health equity under the Affordable Care Act," May 13, 2016. <http://www.hhs.gov/about/news/2016/05/13/hhs-finalizes-rule-to-improve-health-equity-under-affordable-care-act.html>

development,[164] raise serious moral issues about our collective obligation for children's welfare.

My goal is not to debate in detail all the policy issues but rather ask more basic questions about the ideology of transgenderism. That exploration will focus on biological, cultural, and ecological frameworks of analysis, raising a question, a challenge, and a concern.

Question: Biology of Male/Female

If one takes seriously biological sex differences (male and female), then transgender claims are not clear. Confusion starts with the phrase 'their assigned sex at birth' in the definition of a transgender person. That phrase is relevant to intersex people whose sex is ambiguous when doctors may decide to label them as male or female. But 'assigned' implies there is a judgment, and the vast majority of humans are not really assigned a sex category by human choice but rather occupy a sex category, male or female, depending on one's potential role in reproduction and one's sex chromosomes, XX or XY. Yes, some specific person records that designation on a birth certificate, but in the vast majority of cases the 'assignment' of male or female has a clear material basis and is not ambiguous or contested.

---

164 Francine Russo, "Transgender Kids," *Scientific American Mind*, January/ February 2016, pp. 26–35; Priyanka Boghani, "When Transgender Kids Transition, Medical Risks are Both Known and Unknown," PBS Frontline, June 30, 2015. <http://www.pbs.org/wgbh/frontline/article/when-transgender-kids-transition-medical-risks-are-both-known-and-unknown/>; Jake Thomas, "Delaying Puberty with the Help of the State," *The Atlantic*, October 22, 2014. <http://www.theatlantic.com/health/archive/2014/10/delaying-puberty-with-the-help-of-the-state/381366/>

So, if a person says, "I was born male but am actually female," I do not understand what that means in the context of modern understandings of biology. Although not all transgender people describe their experience as "being shipwrecked in the wrong body,"[165] as Jennifer Finney Boylan put it, I struggle to understand the concept, no matter what the metaphor. In that essay, Boylan suggested, "The fact that many nontrans people have never experienced gender dysphoria is offered as proof that it therefore must not exist, in the same way that straight people once dismissed gay humanity because they had never experienced any same-sex desire themselves."

Whatever the accuracy of that claim regarding others, it doesn't describe me. As a child, I struggled with gender norms and sexuality. I was small and effeminate, one of those boys who clearly was not going to be able to 'be a man', as defined in patriarchy. My sexual orientation also was unclear, as I struggled to understand my attraction to males and females, something that could not be openly discussed in the 1970s where I was growing up. And my early life included traumatic experiences that not only further complicated my self-understanding but also left me feeling connected to people who don't fit easily into the dominant culture's categories. While my experience isn't one of 'gender dysphoria' as I understand that diagnostic category, the experiences of transgender people are not hard for me to understand. It is only the explanatory framework that confuses me.

I return to this basic question: If male and female are discernable and definable biological categories, what does it mean for someone born unambiguously male (not intersex) to say, "I am female" or for someone born unambiguously female

---

165 Jennifer Finney Boylan, "Trans Community Can Change Minds by Changing Discourse," *Los Angele Times*, August 15, 2014. <http://www.latimes.com/opinion/op-ed/la-oe-adv-boylan-transgender-language-20140817-story.html>

to say, "I am male"? It's possible that some future scientific inquiry will produce a theory to make sense of that claim, but no such theory exists today, and it's difficult to imagine what such a theory would be. Can one have male characteristics in all parts of the body but have a female brain? That implies that the differences between brains of male and female humans are significant enough to warrant such claims, which is not supported by experience or evidence: "Human brains, unlike genitals, cannot be 'sexed', meaning that they cannot be sorted reliably into 'male-type' and 'female-type' by observers who don't know the sex of the person they came from."[166] A prominent neuroscientist points out that the differences are small and variable: "Knowing information about one of these areas in an individual's brain doesn't allow accurate prediction of the person's sex."[167] At best, claims about these differences are highly speculative,[168] and don't coherently explain transgender identity.

If there is an essence of maleness and femaleness that is non-material, in the spiritual realm, then we are discussing theology, broadly defined. People have a right to make spiritual claims, but they tend to be compelling only to those who share a similar theology. So, if someone claims to have a male body but a female soul, I understand how those terms are being used

---

166 Rebecca Jordan-Young, *Brain Storm: The Flaws in the Science of Sex Differences* (Cambridge, MA: Harvard University Press, 2010), p. 49. See also Rebecca Jordan-Young and Raffaella I. Rumiati, "Hardwired for Sexism? Approaches to Sex/Gender," *Neuroethics*, 5 (2012): 305–315.

167 Robert M. Sapolsky, "Caught Between Male and Female," *Wall Street Journal*, December 6, 2013. <http://www.wsj.com/articles/SB10001424052702304854804579234030532617704>

168 Cordelia Fine, *Delusions of Gender: How Our Minds, Society, and Neurosexism Create Difference* (New York: W.W. Norton and Co., 2010). See also Cordelia Fine, "His brain, her brain?" *Science*, 346 (2014): 915–916.

but don't find any claims about a non-material soul—sexed/gendered or not—to be plausible.

While no one takes Bruce/Caitlyn Jenner to be the spokesperson for the transgender movement, this comment in Jenner's interview with ABC News captures those two common explanations: "My brain is much more female than it is male. It's hard for people to understand that, but that's what my soul is."[169] Whether articulated by a celebrity, activist, or scientist, these kinds of claims—about the material brain or the non-material soul—are difficult to understand.

These questions can't be answered by merely dismissing them. When the Obama administration announced a policy shift on the use of bathrooms in schools, U.S. Attorney General Loretta Lynch argued that guaranteeing access to the bathroom of a transgender person's choice was analogous to ending 'whites only' facilities during the struggle against American apartheid:

> It was not so very long ago that states, including North Carolina, had signs above restrooms, water fountains and on public accommodations keeping people out based upon *a distinction without a difference* (emphasis added). We have moved beyond those dark days, but not without pain and suffering and an ongoing fight to keep moving forward.[170]

Racial categories are indeed a distinction without a difference—we can see the distinction between skin colors but realize the color doesn't create a meaningful difference in people beyond

---

169 "Bruce Jenner: The Interview," ABC News, April 24, 2015. <http://abc.go.com/shows/2020/listing/2015-04/24-bruce-jenner-the-interview>

170 Loretta E. Lynch, "Remarks at Press Conference Announcing Complaint Against the State of North Carolina to Stop Discrimination Against Transgender Individuals," Washington, DC, May 9, 2016. <https://www.justice.gov/opa/speech/attorney-general-loretta-e-lynch-delivers-remarks-press-conference-announcing-complaint>

that imposed by the politics of white supremacy. But the distinction between male and female does make an obvious difference in the act of reproduction, which is essential to the species, and hence can't be waived away rhetorically.

Another troubling question about the body remains: Whether the explanation for gender dysphoria is claimed to be found in science or spirituality, it's not clear how hormonal and surgical interventions in the body could transform a person from one sex category into another. How do manipulations of hormones or genitalia accomplish that shift? Such medical procedures have produced positive results for some transgender people, but that outcome doesn't provide a coherent explanation of the procedures, which leads to confusing claims from many who support the transgender movement. In an article on a prominent liberal website, one writer conflates transgender and intersexed individuals, while mischaracterizing any critique as nothing more than narrow-minded moralism:

> Some females are born with penises and some males are born with vaginas. Some people are even born with both or with ambiguous genitalia. It's just how biology works. It's just human. It may not be the majority, but it's not wrong or bad anymore that being left-handed or having green eyes is wrong or bad.[171]

Those kinds of muddled claims that ignore complex questions do not advance our understanding. I have been asking these questions not to attack the transgender community, but because I cannot make sense of the movement's claims and would like to understand. Our current understanding of

---

171 Karen Dolan, "Caitlyn Jenner Isn't 'Posing' as a Woman—She Is a Woman," *Alternet*, June 1, 2015. <http://www.alternet.org/gender/yes-females-can-have-penises-and-males-can-have-vaginas-get-over-it>

ourselves—biologically and philosophically—does not lead to an obvious answer.

Challenge: Politics of Man/Woman

A final question related to biology: If transgenderism is about a male actually being female, and vice versa, shouldn't the diagnostic category be called 'sex dysphoria' not 'gender dysphoria'? A claim about male/female suggests that such people are not just uncomfortable with the gender norms they are being asked to conform to, but that somehow a definable essence of a person is out of sync with some aspect of one's body. Again, if that is the claim—that there is some set of essential male/female traits that can lead to the wrong sex classification for a person—then it's not that I disagree but that I don't understand it. To me, that account is not like claiming 'two plus two equals five' but more like 'two plus two equals Paris'. The first is incorrect; the second is neither right nor wrong but incoherent given how I understand arithmetic and geography.

But if 'gender dysphoria' involves discomfort with patriarchal gender norms being imposed on people, that's a claim I understand easily, not only from research and the testimony of others but from my own experience. Transgenderism in this sense is about people's experience of being out of sync with the gender norms of their culture. And if gender is socially constructed, then transgenderism is, at its core, a statement of dissatisfaction with a particular social construction of gender in a specific culture at a specific point in history. Since the social construction of any set of norms is influenced by the distribution of power in society, this suggests that challenging the social construction involves political struggle.

The social construction of gender in the contemporary United States occurs in a patriarchal society that generates rigid, repressive, and reactionary gender norms. As I argued in the Sex/Gender chapter, given the centrality of reproduction in the life of any organism, I believe that some gender-role differentiation likely is inevitable given the nature of sex-role differentiation. But there is no 'natural' set of gender norms, beyond the basics of bearing and nursing children. Humans make meaning of male/female biological differences and tell stories about why male and female are different—we create the social categories of masculine/feminine and man/woman—but there is no single way in which we humans can do, or have done, all that. I believe that in decent, stable human communities that transcend patriarchy, gender norms would be limited in scope and flexible, to accommodate individual variation. This position recognizes how little we know about the intellectual/emotional/moral differences that may arise from the biological differences.

Hence, a challenge to the transgender movement: Embrace radical feminism's longstanding resistance to patriarchy. A key component of the second-wave radical feminist movement was a rejection of patriarchal gender norms, especially the demands that women present themselves as attractive to men and be willing to sexually service them, always on men's terms. For women, the benefits of eliminating those norms is obvious. For men, who benefit in some ways from patriarchy, the rejection of gender norms is crucial if we are to be fully human; patriarchal norms pressure men to cut themselves off from anything associated with women, such as caring and emotional vulnerability. While the costs of patriarchal gender norms don't fall equally on women and men, of course, any system that suppresses the ability of people to explore their full humanity is inconsistent with both individual and community flourishing.

Transgenderism could embrace radical feminists' understanding that gender-in-patriarchy—in this society at this moment in history—is a system that established and reinforces inequality in the service of institutionalized male dominance. To resist those patriarchal norms, one does not need to switch gender categories but can, through individual and collective action, refuse to accept the constraints whenever possible and identify with a movement to end patriarchy.

Ironically, men who claim the identity of a woman, or vice versa,[172] are helping to reinforce the rigidity of gender norms by suggesting that to cope with discomfort created by those norms one must switch categories; such an act doesn't challenge patriarchy but instead bolsters patriarchal ideology. This perspective is not new; feminists have been offering similar analyses for decades. For example, psychologist Sandra Bem wrote in the 1990s that transsexualism (the more common term then)

> would be much better conceptualized as a social pathology than as an individual pathology. ... the underside of the same process of gender polarization that also produces highly conventional males and females. In a less gender-polarizing culture, after all, it would matter much less if the individual's personality and behavior did not cohere into a tightly gender-polarized package that matches her or his biological sex. In addition, so much less would be defined as masculine or feminine in the first place that

---

172 Not all people who identify as transgender make this claim. See Michelle Goldberg, "The Trans Women Who Say that Trans Women Aren't Women: Meet the Apostates of the Trans Rights Movement," *Slate*, December 9, 2015. <http://www.slate.com/articles/double_x/doublex/2015/12/gender_critical_trans_women_the_apostates_of_the_trans_rights_movement.single.html>

sex would not so dramatically limit the kind of a person that one could be, and hence people would have much less reason to be desperately unhappy with the particular sex they happened to be born with.[173]

Another contemporary response to a dissatisfaction with gender norms that sometimes is included in discussion of the transgender community is the refusal to be categorized as man or woman, what is typically called the 'genderqueer' position:

> A person whose gender identity is neither man nor woman, is between or beyond genders, or is some combination of genders. This identity is usually related to or in reaction to the social construction of gender, gender stereotypes and the gender binary system. Some genderqueer people identify under the transgender umbrella while others do not.[174]

Related terms include 'non-binary', 'gender variant', 'gender fluid', and 'gender nonconforming', all of which signal a rejection of claims about natural and immutable gender norms. It can be difficult to keep up with the terminology (at Nonbinary.org, the entry for 'multigender' includes more than 25 entries[175]) or sometimes make sense of the rhetoric. For example, a multigender writer claims that there "are at least as many genders as there have been humans who have lived,"[176] which suggests gender can be used as simply another term for an individual human personality.

---

173 Sandra Lipsitz Bem, *The Lenses of Gender: Transforming the Debate on Sexual Inequality* (New Haven, CT: Yale University Press, 1993), p. 111.

174 "Definition of Terms," Gender Equity Resource Center. <http://geneq.berkeley.edu/lgbt_resources_definiton_of_terms#gender_queer>

175 <http://nonbinary.org/wiki/Multigender>

176 Jenny Crofton, "What It Means to Be MultiGender: The Questions Many Have, but Are Afraid to Ask," *The Body Is Not An Apology Magazine*, August 5, 2016. <http://thebodyisnotanapology.com/magazine/what-it-means-to-be-multigender-the-questions-many-have-but-are-afraid-to-ask/>

Again, much of radical feminism has long encouraged people to resist the rigid, repressive, and reactionary gender norms in patriarchy, and to recognize that the norms emerge from a system of power that can be resisted. Any genderqueer or similar position that doesn't foreground a feminist struggle against patriarchy has to offer its own political strategy for ending the violence and discrimination that patriarchy produces.

Concern: Ecological Limits

To repeat a simple but important point: When trying to understand the world, I begin with the recognition that human beings are organisms living in ecosystems, part of a larger living world that we call the ecosphere. Although human cognitive and linguistic capacities are impressive (at least to us, by standards we set), the complexity of the world far outstrips our ability to understand it, and what capacities we have do not allow us to transcend the biophysical limits of the ecosphere.

This ecospheric worldview recognizes that we are complex living creatures existing in a vastly complex world, and that there are limits to both what we can know about that world and how we should attempt to manipulate that world. The modern industrial worldview—dependent on concentrated energy sources to make advanced technology possible—ignores ecological realities and celebrates expansive manipulation. But we have intervened in the living systems of the planet, especially during the fossil-fuel epoch, in ways that have turned out to be enormously destructive. Instead of proceeding with caution and a humility appropriate to our limits, humans have been reckless and arrogant, and hence have not understood the limits for living beings and living systems.[177]

This deeper ecological awareness should make us wary of "technological fundamentalism,"[178] the belief that the use of increasingly sophisticated high-energy, advanced technology is always a good thing and that any problems caused by the unintended consequences of such technology eventually can be remedied by more technology. Those who question such declarations are often said to be 'anti-technology', which is a meaningless term. All human beings use technology of some kind, from stone tools to supercomputers. An anti-fundamentalist position is not that all technology is bad, but that the introduction of new technology should be evaluated carefully regarding the basis of its effects—predictable and unpredictable—on human communities and the non-human world, with an understanding of the limits of our knowledge. One expression of this idea is the "precautionary principle,"[179] an argument for caution in introducing new products or procedures when the consequences are disputed or unknown.

Technological fundamentalism promotes the view that life is an engineering project, whether we are focused on the planet's ecosystems or the systems that make up the human organism. At the core of a more ecological and life-centered approach to humans' place on the planet is respect for the integrity of the body and an awareness that our bodies are governed by the same laws of physics and chemistry as the ecosphere. High-energy/advanced-technology interventions

---

177 Ted Mosquin and Stan Rowe, "A Manifesto for Earth," *Biodiversity*, 5:1 (2004): 3–9. <http://www.ecospherics.net/pages/EarthManifesto.pdf>

178 David W. Orr, "Technological Fundamentalism," *Conservation Biology*, 8:2 (June 1994): 335–337.

179 "Precautionary Principle," Science and Environmental Health Network. <http://www.sehn.org/precaution.html>

into the body should be approached with the same caution and humility that should mark our interventions into the ecosphere.

Elective cosmetic surgery is a good example of the culture's disconnection from that larger living world. All living things eventually die, of course, and human appearance changes as we age. Yet in our high-energy/advanced-technology society, many people search for ways to stave off aging or to change their appearance for other non-medical reasons. In 2014, Americans spent more than $12 billion on 10 million cosmetic procedures (surgical and nonsurgical), 90% of which were performed on women. The two most common surgical procedures, liposuction and breast augmentation,[180] help focus us on important questions.

Liposuction, or lipoplasty, "slims and reshapes specific areas of the body by removing excess fat deposits, improving your body contours and proportion, and ultimately, enhancing your self-image." Breast augmentation, or augmentation mammoplasty, "is the surgical placement of breast implants to increase fullness and improve symmetry of the breasts, or to restore breast volume lost after weight reduction or pregnancy."[181] Although some people who get liposuction are overweight, it is not a treatment for obesity, and breast augmentation is rarely related to physical health. These procedures typically are chosen by people seeking to conform to social norms about appearance.

---

180 "Cosmetic Surgery National Data Bank Statistics," American Society for Aesthetic Plastic Surgery. <http://www.surgery.org/sites/default/files/2014-Stats.pdf>

181 "Cosmetic Procedures," American Society of Plastic Surgeons. <http://www.plasticsurgery.org/cosmetic-procedures.html>

The gender patterns of these surgeries are hard to ignore. While feminists are not of one mind on the subject,[182] some have argued for "the rejection of any cosmetic bodily alternative as violent and unethical" and instead advocate for "continuing work to challenge stereotypical media images of feminine women and masculine men."[183] Combining critiques of technological fundamentalism and patriarchy leads me to conclude that these cosmetic practices are inconsistent with stable, decent communities that promote human flourishing in an ecologically sustainable fashion. The fact that people opt for these procedures, and that some of those people report positive outcomes, doesn't end the conversation about their larger effects. Sheila Jeffreys has argued that in patriarchy, "beauty practices are not about women's individual choice or a 'discursive space' for women's creative expression but, as other radical feminist theorists have argued before me, a most important aspect of women's oppression."[184]

Even just raising a feminist challenge to cosmetic surgery in a conversation about sex-reassignment surgery often leads to charges of transphobia, but the parallels are difficult to ignore. Obviously, not all people who identify as transgender seek hormone therapy or sex-reassignment surgery. But in general the transgender movement embraces these approaches for those who want them, arguing that they should not be questioned and should be publicly funded as medically necessary treatment. Again, while these procedures have positive outcomes for some people, how can a procedure

---

182 Cressida J. Heyes and Meredith Jones, eds., *Cosmetic Surgery: A Feminist Primer* (Farnham, UK: Ashgate Publishing, 2009).

183 Tania Lienert, "Women's Self-Starvation, Cosmetic Surgery and Transsexualism," *Feminism & Psychology*, 8:2 (1998): 245.

184 Sheila Jeffreys, *Beauty and Misogyny: Harmful Cultural Practices in the West* (London: Routledge, 2005), p. 2.

be deemed medically necessary when there is so little understanding of the nature of the condition being corrected, let alone its etiology?

That concern could be trumped by conclusive evidence that the procedures alleviate people's sense of discomfort, distress, and social dislocation, but the evidence is, at best, mixed. One study in Sweden concluded:

> Persons with transsexualism, after sex reassignment, have considerably higher risks for mortality, suicidal behaviour, and psychiatric morbidity than the general population. Our findings suggest that sex reassignment, although alleviating gender dysphoria, may not suffice as treatment for transsexualism, and should inspire improved psychiatric and somatic care after sex reassignment for this patient group.[185]

Other studies found clearer evidence of success, but the few studies involve a small number of patients.[186] A review of twenty-eight studies with 1,833 participants who underwent sex reassignment that included hormonal therapies concluded, "Very low quality evidence suggests that sex reassignment that includes hormonal interventions in individuals with gender identity disorder likely improves gender dysphoria, psychological functioning and comorbidities, sexual function and overall quality of life."[187]

---

185 Cecilia Dhejne, et al., "Long-Term Follow-Up of Transsexual Persons Undergoing Sex Reassignment Surgery: Cohort Study in Sweden," *PLoS One*, 6:2 (2011). <http://journals.plos.org/plosone/article?id=10.1371/journal.pone.0016885>

186 Annelou L.C. de Vries, et al., "Young Adult Psychological Outcome after Puberty Suppression and Gender Reassignment," *Pediatrics*, 134:4 (2014): 696–704. <http://www.ncbi.nlm.nih.gov/pubmed/25201798>

187 Mohammad Hassan Murad, et al., "Hormonal Therapy and Sex Reassignment: A Systematic Review and Meta-analysis of Quality of Life and Psychosocial Outcomes," *Clinical Endocrinology*, 72:2 (2010): 214–231. <http://onlinelibrary.wiley.com/doi/10.1111/j.1365-2265.2009.03625.x/abstract>

For the sake of argument, let's assume sex-reassignment surgery produced demonstrable positive results for the majority of people who underwent the procedure. A more basic question would remain about the implications of such surgery, which destroys healthy tissue rather than repairs diseased or damaged parts of the body. Here's a summary of the types of common procedures, from an advocate for transgender people:

> For adults, chest or breast surgery, genital reconstructive surgery, and facial feminization or masculinization surgery are available. If 18 months or more of feminizing hormone therapy has not resulted in sufficient breast growth, augmentation is available. For transsexual men, the breast can be removed and a male-appearing chest can be created. Genital reconstructive surgery of transsexual women includes orchiectomy (removal of testes), vaginoplasty, and creation of a clitoris. Most common is the penile inversion technique, where the outer skin of the penis becomes the inner lining of the vagina. The glans of the penis is reduced to form a clitoris. The testicles are removed and scrotum tissue is used to create the labia. Genital reconstructive surgery for transsexual men includes hysterectomy, oophorectomy (removal of ovaries), metoidioplasty, or phalloplasty. Metoidioplasty involves release of the clitoris bringing it forward, extension of the urethra so one can stand to void, and creation of a scrotum from the labia with testicle implants inserted. It is a simpler procedure than phalloplasty and does not require an extensive skin graft. For phalloplasty, a skin graft is needed and often is taken from the forearm. For the phallus to become erect, a penile implant is required. Facial surgery is available to feminize or masculinize the appearance of the face, and neck. This may include surgery of the nose, brow bone, cheeks, jaw, chin, and Adam's apple.[188]

---

188 Bockting, "Transgender Identity Development," pp. 751–752.

Another scholar who is also an advocate, reflecting on an even more exhaustive list of these procedures, noted:

> It can seem and feel as if one is *at war with one's body* (emphasis added), reviewing this list of interventions. To make the experience more tolerable, it is imperative to help reframe this process, not with a warfare mentality and vernacular but as a more positive process.[189]

The war metaphor seems appropriate and difficult to simply wish away. Perhaps what drives a desire to make sex-reassignment surgery "more tolerable" is the awareness—whether articulated or not—that when surgeons destroy healthy tissue in these procedures, no one is really sure what is being accomplished medically. It's difficult not to ask, as we should with cosmetic surgery: Is this a healthy way for society to address people's discomfort and distress with social norms, through this kind of intensely invasive medical intervention? That seems like an obvious question, yet in polite liberal company where support for transgenderism is common, it would, again, likely lead to accusations of transphobia.

None of this is a condemnation of any individual who decides on surgery, but rather a concern about the health of the larger culture in which surgery is offered as a solution. We can understand that "[t]ransgender persons have been documented in many indigenous, Western, and Eastern cultures and societies from antiquity until the present day," as the APA factsheet observes, but must also remember to include the next sentence: "However, the meaning of gender nonconformity may vary from culture to culture."[190] Not every

---

189 SJ Langer, "Our Body Project: From Mourning to Creating the Transgender Body," *International Journal of Transgenderism*, 15:2 (2014): 74.

190 "Answers to Your Questions about Transgender People, Gender Identity and Gender Expression," American Psychological Association. <http://www.apa.

culture deals with the question of gender with the hormonal and surgical interventions of a technologically fundamentalist culture.

Yet a leading doctor who endorses this approach appears to have no hesitation, writing of his eagerness to intervene in children's development with 'puberty blockers' at a point when such treatment was not approved in the United States: "[W]e remain at a crossroads, salivating at the prospect of applying the Dutch protocol for pubertal suppression, yet without permission from health insurers to pay for the expensive drugs or pressure from the medical and mental health communities to demand it."[191] Talk of 'salivating' to use a treatment that interrupts the development of children based on limited research and sketchy understanding of the condition being treated is an example of technological fundamentalism and a rejection of an ecological worldview. To be concerned about this rush into medical/technological 'solutions' to a problem that so clearly has important social and political dimensions is not transphobia but a cautious response rooted in humility about what we don't know.

Imagination

I'm often told that my inability to understand transgenderism is a failure of my imagination, that I'm trapped in either the man/woman or the male/female binary, that I can't see past my cisgender privilege. But I don't fit the term 'cisgender'—defined in the Oxford English Dictionary as "a person whose sense of personal identity matches their gender at birth"—for

---

org/topics/lgbt/transgender.aspx>

191 Spack, "Foreword," in *The Transgender Child*, p. xi.

reasons that sum up my position on the concept of transgender. My sense of personal identity does not line up with the gender norms for males in patriarchy; I am a critic of those gender norms and identify with feminist movements that challenge those norms. If someone were to coin the term 'cissex', I would reject that as a label as well, because I don't know what it means when someone born unambiguously biologically male (as I was) claims to be female; the idea of cissex is incoherent in my understanding of biology.

I can easily imagine a world beyond patriarchy in which people develop their capacities unconstrained by rigid, repressive, and reactionary gender norms. In that world, we would not have to ignore the biological reality of a sexually dimorphic species to allow people to flourish in the myriad ways individual humans could live within the reality of that biological male/female binary, unconstrained by patriarchal notions of gender and power.

My imagination functions just fine, but I try not to imagine away complex intellectual questions and difficult social and political problems. When a claim does not make sense to me, I seek clarification, and when others tell me they have similar problems making sense of a claim, I assume there's something important to work out. Based on correspondence and conversations with others and on the discussion going on in the culture at large, the questions, challenges, and concerns raised in this chapter are not unique to me.

As I suggested at the beginning of this chapter, many people in left/progressive/liberal circles mute themselves out of a fear of being called transphobic. As I've talked with more people about this, even more common is another fear—hurting the feelings of transgender people. After summarizing my position to a longtime comrade in feminist and progressive movements, I asked her opinion. She agreed with my analysis, but said that she thought transgender people had enough problems and that she didn't want to seem mean-spirited in raising critical questions.

"So, your solidarity with the transgender movement is based on the belief that the people in the movement aren't emotionally equipped to discuss the intellectual and political assertions they make?" I asked, pointing out that it's a strange basis for solidarity. She shrugged, not arguing the point, but sticking to her intention to avoid the question. Those who make that decision should remember that avoiding questions does not provide answers.

CONCLUSION

I want to return to my invocation of James Baldwin's advice about dealing with terror: "Ain't no place to run. So, you walk toward it. At least that way you'll know what hit you."[192]

Looking back to my encounter with a critique of patriarchy as a new graduate student in 1988, at first I was afraid of a radical feminist analysis that seemed to be a threat, to how I understood the world and how I understood myself. Whatever feminism was, I was fairly sure it was dangerous, a movement that would take something from me.

But the more I read and talked with feminists, the less I feared them and the more I feared the pathology of patriarchy. I realized that feminism was not a threat to men, but a gift to us. Feminism challenged my unearned privilege and status, demanding that I reassess the assumptions I had made about what it means to be a man. None of that was easy. But feminism gave me a way to understand why I had never felt like I was man enough, an anxiety that I was learning most men shared. The dominant conception of masculinity in U.S. culture asserts that men are naturally competitive and aggressive, and being

---

192 James Baldwin, interviewed by Mavis Nicholson, "Mavis on Four" (1987). <https://www.youtube.com/watch?v=3Wht4NSf7E4>

a 'real man' is therefore marked by the struggle for control, conquest, and domination. A man looks at the world, sees what he wants, and takes it.

Feminism, I began to realize, was not only the vehicle for women's liberation but also could give me the tools to stop trying to be the man I had never really wanted to be, to reject the rules for a toxic masculinity that I had been socialized into but never felt comfortable with and often felt threatened by.

I had thought that I was walking toward feminism, which I had been trained to fear. But feminism was the set of ideas that gave me the strength—intellectually and morally—to walk toward patriarchy, which is what truly terrified me.

At the heart of that realization was the work of Andrea Dworkin, the central figure in the feminist anti-pornography struggle. When I first picked up one of Dworkin's books, all I knew was that she was an ugly, man-hating feminist dyke. At least, that's what I thought I knew, what I had 'learned' from reading other people's accounts of her work, but that caricature couldn't survive reading even a page of her writing. I quickly realized how deeply Dworkin loved not only women but men, and I understood that she was challenging us to be the best people we could be, to reject the quest for patriarchal control and embrace the struggle to be fully human.

One of the first things by Dworkin that I read was a speech she gave to a men's group in 1983, "I Want a Twenty-Four-Hour Truce During Which There Is No Rape," which was her response to the common question feminists face, "What do women want from men?" Just give us one day of rest, she said, "one day in which no new bodies are piled up, one day in which no new agony is added to the old."[193] Dworkin wanted

---

193 Andrea Dworkin, *Letters from a War Zone* (Brooklyn, NY: Lawrence Hill Books, 1993), pp. 170–171.

to help men, not just for our sake but to stop men's violence against women. She wanted an end to the harassment, rape, battery, child sexual assault, and she knew that required men to change, that we had to recognize that feminism offered us a way to save ourselves. In that same speech, she challenged men to take that responsibility:

> We do not want to do the work of helping you to believe in your humanity. We cannot do it anymore. We have always tried. We have been repaid with systematic exploitation and systematic abuse. You are going to have to do this yourselves from now on and you know it.[194]

I was unsure of what it would mean to believe in my own humanity as a man raised in patriarchy, but it became clear that it meant much more than simply not being a rapist, or not being the worst kind of 'macho shithead'. I understood that the 'sensitive guy' profile I had been cultivating wasn't a free pass out of being critiqued by feminists. Later, when I realized that as a young boy I had been used in the way that girls and women are so often used, the feminist critique of violence and abuse in patriarchy began resonating in me at another level, not simply as someone trained in the role of potential perpetrator but as someone who also had been a victim. I kept following my intellectual and emotional reactions—both of which were telling me that this analysis was intellectually compelling and important to my own survival—and I kept stumbling forward.

As I stumbled, I was lucky to meet Jim Koplin, an older man with extensive experience in feminism and other radical political movements, who became a great friend and guide.[195] I was also fortunate to have a professor, philosopher Naomi

---

194 *Ibid.*, p. 170.

195 I tell the story of that relationship in *Plain Radical: Living, Loving, and Learning to Leave the Planet Gracefully* (Berkeley, CA: Counterpoint/Soft Skull, 2015).

Scheman, as a role model for rigorous and principled intellectual work, and to be part of a vibrant feminist study group with other graduate students. And as I was reading and thinking in the classroom, I got involved in a local feminist education group, Organizing Against Pornography,[196] which grounded me in the community with activist women.

This was a time when radical feminism was an important part of the cultural conversation about sex/gender politics, and while I was under no illusion that the end of patriarchy was just around the corner, I assumed that feminist organizing could contribute to a transformation of a profoundly unjust and fundamentally unsustainable society in the time available. Today, I am no longer so sure of that, for two reasons.

First, in the quarter-century that I have participated in feminist organizing, I have observed the widespread rejection of radical feminism's analysis and insights. While I never thought that mainstream society would rush to embrace those ideas, I would not have predicted how thoroughly they would be ignored, not only in the mainstream but also in large segments of feminism. The literary critic Fredric Jameson wrote, "Someone once said that it is easier to imagine the end of the world than to imagine the end of capitalism,"[197] and I used to joke that for some it may be easier to imagine the end of the world than to imagine the end of air conditioning, as a challenge to affluent society's high-energy/advanced-technology obsessions. But I've come to think that it is far more difficult for most people to imagine the end of patriarchy. The rejection of radical feminism's insights—especially on the

---

196 Organizing Against Pornography, "Organizational Records," Minnesota Historical Society. <http://www2.mnhs.org/library/findaids/00183.xml>

197 Fredric Jameson, "Future City," *New Left Review*, May-June 2003. <http:// newleftreview.org/II/21/fredric-jameson-future-city>

questions of rape, sexual exploitation, and transgenderism, not only in the dominant culture but within feminism—is an indication of how deeply woven into the fabric of everyday life patriarchy is. Radical feminism offers a blunt assessment of patriarchy and demands that we work for dramatic changes— not only in public policy but in our personal lives and ways of thinking about ourselves. That highlights the limits of liberal individualism and of postmodern posturing, which are less demanding and hence more popular. Radical feminism asks a lot of us, politically and personally.

Second, my estimation of the time available for the systemic change needed—to transcend not only patriarchy, but also white supremacy, nationalism, capitalism, and the industrial model for human domination of the planet—has shrunk dramatically. I used to think in terms of a century or two available to us, but now I think in terms of decades, if we are lucky. No one can predict how long the planet's ecosystems can sustain large-scale human societies, but there are good reasons to think that we have for too long been unjustifiably optimistic.

Does that seem unwarranted, maybe even hysterical? Pick any crucial measure of the health of the ecosphere on which our lives depend—groundwater depletion, topsoil loss, chemical contamination, increased toxicity in our own bodies, the number and size of 'dead zones' in the oceans, accelerating extinction of species and reduction of bio-diversity—and the news is bad and getting worse, often at rates of degradation much faster than scientists have expected. We live in an oil-based world that is rapidly depleting the cheap and easily accessible oil,[198] which means we face a huge reconfiguration

---

198 Michael T. Klare, *The Race for What's Left: The Global Scramble for the World's Last Resources* (New York: Metropolitan, 2012).

of the infrastructure that undergirds our lives.[199] Meanwhile, the desperation to avoid that reconfiguration has brought us to the era of 'extreme energy' using even more dangerous and destructive technologies (hydrofracturing, deep-water drilling, tar sands extraction). And, of course, there is the undeniable trajectory of climate disruption.[200]

Scientists have identified tipping points[201] and planetary boundaries[202] that indicate how contemporary human activity is pushing the planet beyond its limits. One prestigious group of scientists has warned that humans likely are forcing a planetary-scale critical transition "with the potential to transform Earth rapidly and irreversibly into a state unknown in human experience," which means that "the biological resources we take for granted at present may be subject to rapid and unpredictable transformations within a few human generations."[203] That's an academically respectable way of saying that without radical change in the way we live immediately, it's game-over for a lot of the life on this planet, including us.

This is the point where progressive activists love to quote Martin Luther King, Jr.: "Let us realize that the arc of the moral universe is long, but it bends toward justice."[204] Even if

---

199 James Howard Kunstler, *The Long Emergency: Surviving the End of Oil, Climate Change, and Other Converging Catastrophes of the Twenty-First Century* (New York: Grove, 2006).

200 Naomi Klein, *This Changes Everything: Capitalism vs. The Climate* (New York: Simon & Schuster, 2014).

201 "Back to Earth," *Nature*, June 7, 2012. <http://www.nature.com/nature/journal/v486/n7401/index.html>

202 "Planetary Boundaries," *Nature*, September 23, 2009. <http://www.nature.com/news/specials/planetaryboundaries/index.html>

203 Anthony Barnosky, et al., "Approaching a State Shift in Earth's Biosphere," *Nature*, June 7, 2012. <http://www.nature.com/nature/journal/v486/n7401/full/nature11018.html>

204 Martin Luther King, Jr., "Where Do We Go from Here?" Annual Report to the Southern Christian Leadership Conference, August 16, 1967. <http://www.

that hopeful assessment of the long-term moral trajectory of the human species is accurate, at this moment in history the rate of bending appears to be far slower than the intensifying rate of ecosphere degradation. How long will we have to keep working at bending the moral arc? Again, no one can predict, but an honest reading of the evidence suggests that optimistic assumptions made by movements in previous eras are no longer tenable.

I was slow to confront these realities, but eventually I abandoned my denial strategies—which were based mostly on the childlike idea that magical solutions would appear because we want them—and began to face the data about the profoundly destructive consequences of our 'way of life' and the painful reality that capitalism's commitment to unchecked greed and unlimited growth is ecocidal. I had never been attracted to religious fundamentalist promises of divine guidance for the chosen, and I gave up the technological fundamentalism that promises that high-energy/advanced-technology gadgets will save us all. Honest engagement with reality is all that is left.

Many people tell me that talking honestly about the multiple, cascading ecological crises is depressing, too much for them to handle. I certainly feel that way some days, but one of the things that prepared me to face difficult ecological realities was my study of pornography. That may seem an odd claim: How can studying sexually explicit material lead to greater willingness to consider ecological collapse? The answer is simple: Because pornography is what the end of the world looks like.

I started using that phrase during public talks on the subject. To engage the audience, I would ask them to shout

stanford.edu/group/King/publications/speeches/Where_do_we_go_from_here.html>

out ways to complete the sentence, "Pornography is …" which helped me assess a group's understanding of sexually explicit material. The responses ranged from "hot" to "degrading to women," and everything in between. After their responses, I would explain that after many years of research on the issue, my answer was: Pornography is what the end of the world looks like.[205]

By that I don't mean that pornography is going to bring about the end of the world, or that pornography is the most threatening social problem we face. But if we have the courage to look honestly at contemporary pornography, we get a glimpse—in a very visceral fashion—of the consequences of the pathology of patriarchy. Much of contemporary pornography is not just sex on film, but sex enacted within the domination/subordination dynamic of patriarchy, presented to mostly male consumers who use it primarily as a masturbation facilitator. As pornography has become more widely available and accepted in mainstream society, it also has become more overtly cruel and degrading to women and more overtly racist. While there is considerable variation in graphic sexually explicit material, the popular gonzo genre pushes the boundaries of the degradation of, and cruelty toward, women. Beyond that extreme material produced by the 'legitimate' pornography industry are even harsher genres—rape porn, torture porn, porn that sexualizes every inequality you can imagine.

At its core, that's what pornography does: It makes inequality sexually arousing. Pornography fuses male dominance with men's sexual pleasure. Pornography eroticizes not only female subordination but every inequality imaginable, most notably the racial inequality in white supremacy. Pornography turns

---

205 For a more extensive explanation, see Robert Jensen, "Pornography Is What the End of the World Looks Like," in Karen Boyle, ed., *Everyday Pornography* (New York: Routledge, 2010), pp. 105–113.

women into objectified bodies for men's sexual pleasure, alienating men from women and men from themselves.

If we look honestly at pornography, we see a world in which empathy and compassion—the emotions that make stable, decent human communities possible—are overwhelmed by a self-centered, emotionally detached pleasure-seeking. Contemporary pornography works only if men repress their ability to empathize with, and feel compassion for, the women being used in the film.

Imagine this kind of abandonment of our own humanity playing out on all fronts in a society structured by multiple hierarchies in which a domination/subordination dynamic shapes virtually all relationships and interaction. Empathy and compassion do not by themselves provide a political analysis, but no decent politics is possible without those emotional capacities. What would the result of those kinds of political and social forces look like? Pornography gives us a picture of such a world, and it is not a world I want to live in.

Does that seem unwarranted or hysterical? Consider the commonplace genres in contemporary pornography, which includes films in which men thrust their penises down women's throats aggressively with the goal of making women gag, or the various kinds of multiple-penetration films in which three men penetrate a woman orally, vaginally, and anally at the same time. The only problem the pornography industry has is figuring out what to do next. As one successful pornography producer told me in an interview at the annual pornography convention, predicting future trends in pornography is difficult because every sexual act we can imagine, no matter how extreme, had already been filmed. "The thing about it is, there's only but so many holes, only but so many different types of penetration that can be executed upon a woman," he said.

After facing the way the pornography industry undermines human flourishing in the most intimate spaces of our lives—facing what is 'normal' in contemporary patriarchy—I was less resistant to facing the consequences of the same dynamic at a global level. In pornography, women are a collection of holes to be filled by the men in the film, so that men at home can masturbate to images of eroticized male domination. Male viewers, who might feel a connection to specific real women, need not worry about how a mere collection of holes might feel; empathy is not a relevant consideration. At the global level, we might feel a connection to specific places in the living world but we need not worry about a world that is defined as either a mine from which we extract the resources we want or a landfill into which we dump our waste.

From the intimate to the global, we live in a world built on domination and subordination, the ultimate expression of which is a claim of ownership. Men claim that they own their women, or at least can buy women for sex when needed, and we humans routinely claim that we can own the larger living world. In the quest for domination through ownership, we eliminate the humanity of those we dominate and treat the world we dominate as if it were nothing but a collection of things we can take. From the intimate to the global, the domination/subordination dynamic is terrifying.

But rather than be paralyzed by that terror, I'm trying to walk toward it. The dominant culture's fear of assessing honestly the unjust and unsustainable nature of modern systems may mean that our moral arc can't bend fast enough to prevent the worst of what's coming, but that doesn't mean there is nothing to be done, that no projects are worth our time and energy. This brings me back to the question I posed earlier that I think can guide our choices about political projects: "Is this likely to help people create and maintain stable, decent human communities that can remain in a sustainable relationship with the larger living world?"

That question need not imply that working to create such communities will prevent the worst of what may be coming, but instead can remind us that whatever is coming we will need to hold onto core values. Even if we can't change the trajectory of this unjust and unsustainable society, we can strive to be part of a saving remnant, holding onto the concepts of dignity (all people come into the world with the same moral claim to a fulfilling life), solidarity (humans are social beings who thrive when living in meaningful relationships within a community), and equality (a rough parity of resources is necessary to honor the dignity claim and make solidarity meaningful).

These values, central to feminism and other radical analyses, animate my vision of a saving remnant, the preservation of communities, however small they may be, that could be stable over time and foster decent values that enhance human flourishing in a sustainable relationship with the larger living world.

If that seems impossible to imagine, because patriarchy and other systems that are based on domination/subordination dynamic seem too overwhelming, let me offer a metaphor that I first encountered in a class with Naomi Scheman, the feminist philosopher who had such an influence on my intellectual development. Think of patriarchy as being like concrete in the city, Scheman suggested. It covers almost everything, heavy and seemingly unmovable, paving over the life of the non-human world. But the daily wear and tear produces cracks, and in those cracks plants can grow—a little grass here and there, some weeds, sometimes even a flower. Living things have no business growing through concrete but they do, resisting the concrete's attempt to define the city.

That's where the action is, in the cracks of patriarchy, white supremacy, nationalism, capitalism, the industrial model that worships high-energy/advanced-technology. It is in those cracks that we can nurture dignity, solidarity, equality. Making a serious commitment to working in those cracks does not require arrogant claims that we know how to solve all problems, or that a single ideology can provide solutions, or that large-scale solutions are possible in the time available to us. But we can, with the humility that emerges from a recognition of human limits, commit to resisting any ideas, systems, institutions, and practices that are based on the claim that a domination/subordination dynamic is natural or inevitable. We can commit to resisting any ideology that reduces any human being to the status of an object or refuses to respect the integrity of the human body as part of a larger living world.

With that approach to social change in mind, I continue to believe radical feminism offers a productive framework for understanding 'the social construction of gender' that in patriarchy produces inequality: (1) the parameters of our actions are defined by biological realities of a sexually dimorphic species with sex differences that are independent of human judgment, but humans make judgments about what meaning to assign to those differences; (2) we make individual choices but those choices are conditioned by the opportunities available to people and constraints placed on them, as they understand these things at a given moment in history in a particular place; and (3) the choices we make, individually and collectively, must be consistent not only with principles of social justice but also with the biophysical limits of the larger living world.

I believe that these ideas are central to the liberation of women in patriarchy and to men's project of claiming our humanity, as well as to the struggle to create stable, decent human communities. I believe that this project requires not only new ways of organizing ourselves socially, politically, and economically, but a different way of understanding what it means to be human.

I do not speak for feminist women, let alone for women more generally. I do not speak for feminist men, let along for men more generally. I'm not telling anyone else how they must understand the world. I am trying to articulate, as clearly as possible, how I have come to understand the world through an engagement with feminism and other radical critiques of illegitimate authority, and why I believe those understandings are important to our individual and collective flourishing.

I am not optimistic that existing critical movements will be successful in leading the radical transformation necessary, but I do not hesitate to endorse radical approaches to achieving social justice and ecological sustainability and look for creative ways to advance those goals. Whatever we can or cannot accomplish in the coming decades, we can try our best to live according to the values we claim to hold and to make changes where we can.

The only thing I am reasonably sure about is that all of this is painful, and we should be grateful for the ability to feel that pain, which is a sign that we are alive and struggling to be more fully human. As I approach the age of sixty, my life cleaves neatly into two halves. For the first half, I desperately tried to be 'normal', to fit in, to be a man, to be 'realistic' about how the world worked—and it left me miserable. In the second half of my life, I have tried to understand the sources of that misery, both in the particularities of my own circumstances and in the systems that structure our society, trying to stay true to the pledge to be honest in my assessment of how the world works and self-critical about my own life. That process has often been, and continues to be, painful, yet I have no intention of going back.

I do not believe there is some magical virtue in pain, that suffering automatically makes us more virtuous. Pain simply is part of any human life, and the question is how we deal with suffering. Do we run from it, or walk toward it?

Better than any contemporary writer I know, James Baldwin understood these decisions. In 1962, writing about the role of artists in helping a society, such as white-supremacist America, face the depth of its pathology, he reminded us, "Not everything that is faced can be changed; but nothing can be changed until it is faced." In that essay, titled "As Much Truth as One Can Bear,"[206] Baldwin suggested that a great writer attempts "to tell as much of the truth as one can bear, and then a little more."

I would extend Baldwin's challenge by another step. Our task—for all of us, men and women, in whatever endeavors we have chosen—is to tell as much of the truth as we can bear, and then a little more, and then all the rest of the truth, whether we can bear it or not.

The truth—of the pathology of patriarchy and other domination/subordination dynamics within the human family, and of the human failure to understand our place in the larger living world—is more than we should have to bear, maybe more than we can bear, and yet bearing it is our task. To turn away from that task is to turn away from our own humanity.

---

206 James Baldwin, "As Much Truth As One Can Bear," in Randall Kenan, ed., *The Cross of Redemption: Uncollected Writings* (New York: Pantheon, 2010), pp. 28–34.

Afterword

ON FEAR AND RESISTANCE

by Rebecca Whisnant [207]

I n her 1975 speech "The Sexual Politics of Fear and Courage,"
Andrea Dworkin argued that fear shapes and constrains the
lives of women under male supremacy. "As women," she said,

> we learn fear as a function of our so-called femininity. We are
> taught systematically to be afraid, and we are taught that to be
> afraid not only is congruent with femininity, but inheres in it.
> We are taught to be afraid so that we will not be able to act, so
> that we will be passive, so that we will be women ...[208]

---

207 Rebecca Whisnant is Associate Professor and Chair of the Philosophy
Department at the University of Dayton. She is co-editor (with Christine
Stark) of *Not For Sale: Feminists Resisting Prostitution and Pornography* and
(with Peggy DesAutels) *Global Feminist Ethics*. She has published numerous
articles on sexual violence and exploitation, and is vice president of the board of
Culture Reframed, a national nonprofit organization combatting pornography
as a public health crisis.

208 Andrea Dworkin, "The Sexual Politics of Fear and Courage," in *Our Blood:
Prophecies and Discourses on Sexual Politics* (New York: Perigee Books, 1976),
p. 55.

This fear, Dworkin went on to say, is isolating, confusing, and debilitating. It deforms the female personality and prevents women from understanding and organizing against our oppression.

The theme of fear looms large in this book. Robert Jensen knows, as well as a man can know, the distinctively 'feminine' fear that Dworkin describes. As he shows in his chapter on rape culture, the fear of male violence shapes women's everyday interactions with men, from sexual relationships to passing encounters on the street. He describes, too, the fear of other men and boys—and of not measuring up as a man—that plagued his own early life. In short, within patriarchy, both women and men are deathly afraid of men, and rightly so.

For Jensen, however, while fear can constrain and debilitate, it can also yield analysis that then motivates and directs. As we come to feminist consciousness, and especially to radical feminist consciousness, we begin to understand all too well what there is to be afraid of. We see the same things as before, but we see them differently—as results of a destructive and life-hating system called patriarchy, with its multiple offshoots of racism, imperialism, capitalism, and environmental catastrophe. In Jensen's view, we would be foolish *not* to be afraid of the multiple crises that cruelly constrain our lives and that now threaten our survival as a species—and of the systems that produce those crises. But fear can be a revolutionary force, Jensen contends, so long as we follow James Baldwin's advice to walk *toward* what is scaring us. At least, as Baldwin put it, that way we'll know what hit us. Furthermore, as feminist philosopher Sandra Bartky once observed, there is a certain freedom in coming to feminist consciousness—fear and all: "No longer do we have to practice on ourselves that mutilation of intellect and personality required of individuals who, caught up in an irrational and destructive system, are nevertheless not allowed to regard it as anything but sane, progressive, and normal."[209]

Beginning with the Body

Robert Jensen opens the book by naming its origin: "This book began in my body ..." His own bodily reactions—to fear, to anxiety and uncertainty, to a feeling of 'rightness' as critical awareness gradually took shape—guided him to a radical feminist understanding of his own life and of the world.

The centrality of the body to his own political awakening, and to the analysis that unfolds from that awakening, places Jensen within a rich tradition of radical feminist thought and practice. Radical feminists have long known that an understanding of patriarchy often begins with the most intimate spaces of our lives. In the process of feminist consciousness-raising (whatever its culturally and historically specific forms), women learn together to, in Jensen's words, "pay attention to our emotional, embodied life and what it teaches us." For many women who become radical feminists, awareness dawns when we begin to see our bodily experiences—from menstruation and childbirth to rape, abortion, domestic labor, and more—as politically meaningful. Rather than dismissing those experiences, and our feelings about them, as trivial or merely personal, we come to put them in an analytical context that both clarifies and liberates, not least by connecting us with other women. (As Jensen's correspondent Lisa puts it, "I do need to know that I'm not completely alone ... I think that there are probably a lot of me.")

---

209 Sandra Bartky, "Toward a Phenomenology of Feminist Consciousness," in *Femininity and Domination: Studies in the Phenomenology of Oppression* (New York: Routledge, 1990), p. 21.

Furthermore, radical feminism's moral and political core is the demand, directly counter to patriarchal dictates and practices, for female bodily sovereignty. Jensen's analysis echoes this demand, from his elucidation of rape culture to his opposition to industries of sexual exploitation. As he shows, in both contexts "patriarchy defines women's sexuality as the thing that men take ..." In contrast, to claim bodily sovereignty for women and girls is simply to claim our full humanity. That such a claim is, indeed, *still* radical underlines how far we are from that status.

Robert Jensen's focus on the body also helps explain one area where he diverges from many radical feminists— namely, his skepticism regarding gender abolition. In the words of one radical feminist organization, WoLF (Women's Liberation Front), "gender is a hierarchical caste system that organizes male supremacy. Gender cannot be reformed—it must be abolished."[210] In contrast, Jensen doubts whether total abolition of all gendered roles, norms, traits, and symbolism is a realistic or even desirable goal. While he agrees that gender as we know it is a destructive hierarchy, he believes that pre-patriarchal societies have had, and post-patriarchal societies could have, different and better ways to make sense of and respond to human maleness and femaleness. Precisely because of the sexual and reproductive dimorphism of human bodies, and the inevitable importance of those bodily differences within human lives and societies, Jensen argues, "we will live with some kind of gender stories, and our task is to strive for gender roles and norms that foster rather than impede stable, decent human communities."

---

210 Women's Liberation Front, "WOLF statement of principles," n.d. <http://womensliberationfront.org/wolf-key-documents/>

People Called Women [211]

A concern about bodies, their treatment, and their categorization also animates Jensen's foray into the highly fraught debates around feminism and transgender politics. It is fair to say that the questions typically asked by radical feminists in this area have not been welcome in broader feminist and progressive circles. In fact, for many people, the only context in which they have encountered the concept of radical feminism is as part of the derogatory acronym TERF ('transexclusionary radical feminism')—itself often embedded in a stream of vitriol and misrepresentation of the persons and politics so characterized.

Much of the conflict has centered on the inclusion of transwomen in women's spaces and endeavors—from music festivals, sports teams, and dormitories to colleges, bathrooms, and conferences. Except for noting their existence—and the need to ground them in rationally defensible accounts of transgenderism itself—Jensen stays away from the specifics of these debates. Rather, the core issue in his discussion is whether "the transgender movement provides a politically productive route to challenging patriarchy." His answer, clearly, is that it does not.

Some readers who otherwise agree with Jensen may have struggled with this chapter. Such struggle is worthwhile so long as it contributes to continued thought and debate. As a

---

211 The phrase comes from a quote by Andrea Dworkin, who wrote the following in her essay "Against the male flood:" "Silence is not speech. We have silence, not speech. We fight rape, battery, incest, and prostitution with it. We lose. But someday someone will notice: that people called women were buried in a long silence that meant dissent and that the pornographers—with needles set in like the teeth of a harrow—chattered on." In *Letters from a War Zone* (Brooklyn, NY: Lawrence Hill Books, 1993), p. 270. People Called Women is also the name of a feminist bookstore in Toledo, Ohio.

supplement to Jensen's valuable discussion, let me briefly address why, as radical feminists, we even care about this issue. What's it to us? Why do we insist on asking questions that put us out of step with the progressive/left/feminist mainstream? Why not say, with British feminist journalist and author Caitlin Moran, "Everybody's welcome in the Lady Party ... pull up a chair"?[212]

As it turns out, the reasons for resisting the Moran approach—appealingly cheerful though it is—go to the heart of radical feminism itself. Radical feminists, after all, claim that women and girls, as a class, are oppressed on the basis of our biology; our female bodies mark us as members of the class of persons to be subjugated. Male control and exploitation of the female body—in particular, its sexual and reproductive capacities—is central to the system of oppression that subordinates females to males. From rape, battering and prostitution to forced childbirth, forced sterilization, female genital mutilation, harmful beauty practices, and much more, the female body is the target of contempt, abuse, and rigid control from birth to old age.

Furthermore, according to radical feminists, feminism exists in order to free women from male domination. That is, the class 'women' is the constituency of feminism, the group of people whose liberation we aim to bring about; feminism is *for* women. And finally, in our view, feminism should be defined, shaped, and led primarily by women; feminism must be centrally not only for women, but *of and by* women.

If the female body and its treatment is at the center of patriarchy itself, and the class 'women' is both the constituency and the prime agent of feminist thought and action, then it

---

212 Quoted in Anna North, "Why feminism can't afford to ignore transgender women" (2013). <https://www.buzzfeed.com/annanorth/why-feminism-cant-afford-to-ignore-transgender-wo?utm_term=.ni4KNJ5xX#.lxQ1wgMkN>

is vital to define clearly what womanhood is. To do so in a way that prioritizes the thoughts and feelings of persons born male, as 'gender identity' approaches do, undermines radical feminism at its core. As the feminist philosopher Jane Clare Jones puts it:

> For feminist women, the axiom 'trans women are women,' when understood to mean 'womanhood *is* gender identity and hence, trans women are women in *exactly the same way* as non-trans women are women' is experienced as an extreme erasure of the way our being-as-women is marked by a system of patriarchal violence that aims to control our sexed bodies.[213]

Again, this perspective, and any resulting hesitation to welcome male-born persons (who identify as women) into the constituency of feminism and into specifically female spaces and endeavors, is widely viewed as rooted in ignorance and bigotry. As a result, as Jensen observes, "many people in left/progressive/liberal circles mute themselves out of a fear of being called transphobic." Yet this is one more area where it is vital not to let our fears—this time, of hostility from those who are in other areas our allies—control or deter us. Jensen has done us a service in opening up avenues for productive discussion, free of malice and name-calling, rooted in the values central to our politics and to the kind of world we aim to create.

---

213 Jane Clare Jones, "'You are killing me': On hate speech and feminist silencing," *Trouble and Strife*, May 6, 2015. <http://www.troubleandstrife.org/new-articles/you-are-killing-me/>

From Fear to Resistance

In this book, Robert Jensen has outlined an understanding of the world that we ignore at our peril. He builds on decades of work by the women who developed radical feminist thought, and further develops a proud tradition of radical feminist publishing from Spinifex Press (including such earlier volumes as *Radically Speaking*, *Not For Sale*, *Big Porn Inc*, and many more). From my own years of work with Robert Jensen as a trusted colleague, I know that he both honors and has been deeply shaped by the brave and groundbreaking work of female radical feminists past and present.

One of my only elements of disagreement with Jensen concerns his subtitle, "Radical Feminism for Men." My disagreement does not concern whether men can be radical feminists or whether they should participate in radical feminist theorizing and action, although both are live questions for some radical feminists. Rather, I see Jensen's work here as an essential framing and defense of radical feminism for everyone, women as well as men. Indeed, he gives men the tools to reject toxic masculinity. But as much as men need radical feminism, women need it even more; our bodily integrity and our basic human dignity are on the line. Thus, I hope that both men *and* women will read and discuss *The End of Patriarchy*.

Toward the end of "The Sexual Politics of Fear and Courage," Andrea Dworkin asks a provocative series of questions:

> How can we, women, who have been taught to be afraid of every little noise in the night, dare to imagine that we might destroy the world that men defend with their armies and their lives? How can we, women, who have no vivid memory of ourselves as heroes, imagine that we might succeed in building a

revolutionary community? Where can we find the revolutionary courage to overcome our slave fear?[214]

As Robert Jensen has demonstrated, courage need not take the place of fear, but can and must exist alongside it. And our fear need not be 'slave fear'—silent, inward-looking, paralyzing; it can and must be revolutionary fear.

As radical feminists, we fear the destructive and hierarchical systems that dictate the terms of our everyday lives. We fear the anger and the violence of men. We fear backlash from mainstream sources and painful conflict with some of our closest friends and allies. All of these fears have something important to teach us, if we will walk toward them, and none of them can deter us from acting on our best understanding of what is true and right. If we are to be revolutionaries for the values of human dignity, solidarity, and equality that Jensen so eloquently defends, we will have to be fearful ones; if we wait until we are unafraid, it will be too late.

References

Sandra Bartky, "Toward a phenomenology of feminist consciousness," in *Femininity and Domination: Studies in the phenomenology of oppression* (New York: Routledge, 1990).

Andrea Dworkin, "The sexual politics of fear and courage," in *Our Blood: Prophecies and discourses on sexual politics* (New York: Perigee Books, 1976).

Andrea Dworkin, "Against the male flood: Censorship, pornography, and equality," in *Letters from a war zone* (Brooklyn, NY: Lawrence Hill Books, 1993).

---

214 Andrea Dworkin, "The Sexual Politics of Fear and Courage," p. 62.

Jane Clare Jones, "'You are killing me': On hate speech and feminist silencing." Retrieved from <http://www.troubleandstrife.org/new-articles/you-are-killing-me/> (2015).

Anna North, "Why feminism can't afford to ignore transgender women." Retrieved from <https://www.buzzfeed.com/annanorth/why-feminism-cant-afford-to-ignore-transgender-wo?utm_term=.ni4KNJ5xX#.lxQ1wgMkN> (2013).

Women's Liberation Front, "WoLF statement of principles." Retrieved from <http://womensliberationfront.org/document-statement-of-principles/> (n.d.)

FURTHER READING

Kathleen Barry, *The Prostitution of Sexuality* (New York: New York University Press, 1995).

Kathleen Barry, *Unmaking War Remaking Men: How Empathy Can Reshape Our Politics, Our Soldiers and Ourselves* (Santa Rosa, CA: Phoenix Rising Press, 2010; North Melbourne, Australia: Spinifex Press 2010).

Diane Bell and Renate Klein, eds., *Radically Speaking: Feminism Reclaimed* (North Melbourne, Australia: Spinifex Press, 1996).

Judith M. Bennett, *History Matters: Patriarchy and the Challenge of Feminism* (Philadelphia: University of Pennsylvania Press, 2006).

Claudia Card, *Lesbian Choices* (New York: Columbia University Press, 1995).

Dorothy Sue Cobble, Linda Gordon, and Astrid Henry, *Feminism Unfinished: A Short, Surprising History of American Women's Movements* (New York: Liveright/W.W. Norton and Co., 2014).

Patricia Hill Collins, *Black Feminist Thought: Knowledge, Consciousness, and the Politics of Empowerment* (New York: Routledge Classics, 2008).

Gail Dines, *Pornland: How Porn Hijacked Our Sexuality* (Boston: Beacon, 2010; North Melbourne, Australia: Spinifex Press, 2010).

Andrea Dworkin, *Pornography: Men Possessing Women* (New York: Dutton, 1989).

Andrea Dworkin, *Letters from a War Zone* (Brooklyn, NY: Lawrence Hill Books, 1993).

Andrea Dworkin, *Heartbreak: The Political Memoir of a Feminist Militant* (New York: Basic Books, 2002).

Judy Foster with Marlene Derlet, *Invisible Women of Prehistory: Three Million Years of Peace, Six Thousand Years of War* (North Melbourne, Australia: Spinifex Press, 2013).

Marilyn Frye, *The Politics of Reality* (Freedom, CA: Crossing Press, 1983).

Marilyn Frye, *Willful Virgin: Essays in Feminism 1976–1992* (Freedom, CA: Crossing Press, 1992).

Sarah Lucia Hoagland, *Lesbian Ethics: Toward New Values* (Palo Alto, CA: Institute of Lesbian Studies, 1989).

bell hooks, *Feminist Theory: From Margin to Center* (Boston: South End Press, 1984).

Sheila Jeffreys, *The Idea of Prostitution* (North Melbourne, Australia: Spinifex Press, 1997).

Sheila Jeffreys, *Beauty and Misogyny: Harmful Cultural Practices in the West* (London: Routledge, 2005).

Allan G. Johnson, *The Gender Knot: Unraveling Our Patriarchal Legacy* (Philadelphia, PA: Temple University Press, 2014, 3rd edition).

Gerda Lerner, *The Creation of Patriarchy* (New York: Oxford University Press, 1986).

Gerda Lerner, *Why History Matters: Life and Thought* (New York: Oxford University Press, 1997).

Audre Lorde, *Sister Outsider* (Freedom, CA: Crossing Press, 1984).

Catharine A. MacKinnon, *Feminism Unmodified: Discourses on Life and Law* (Cambridge, MA: Harvard University Press, 1987).

Catharine A. MacKinnon, *Toward a Feminist Theory of the State* (Cambridge, MA: Harvard University Press, 1989).

Catharine A. MacKinnon and Andrea Dworkin, *In Harm's Way: The Pornography Civil Rights Hearings* (Cambridge, MA: Harvard University Press, 1997).

Cherríe Moraga and Gloria E. Anzaldúa, eds, *This Bridge Called My Back: Writing by Radical Women of Color* (Albany, NY: State University of New York Press, 2015, 4th edition).

Rachel Moran, *Paid for: My Journey through Prostitution* (New York: W.W. Norton and Co., 2015: North Melbourne, Australia: Spinifex Press, 2013).

Caroline Norma and Melinda Tankard Reist, eds., *Prostitution Narratives: Stories of Survival in the Sex Trade* (North Melbourne, Australia: Spinifex Press, 2016).

Peggy Reeves Sanday, *Fraternity Gang Rape: Sex, Brotherhood, and Privilege on Campus* (New York: New York University Press, 1990).

Melinda Tankard Reist and Abigail Bray, eds., *Big Porn Inc: Exposing the Harms of the Global Pornography Industry* (North Melbourne, Australia: Spinifex Press, 2011).

Naomi Scheman, *Engenderings: Constructions of Knowledge, Authority, and Privilege* (New York: Routledge, 1993).

Michael Schwalbe, *Manhood Acts: Gender and the Practices of Domination* (New York: Routledge, 2014).

Barbara Smith, ed., *Home Girls: A Black Feminist Anthology* (New Brunswick, NJ: Rutgers University Press, 2000).

Joyce Trebilcot, *Dyke Ideas: Process, Politics, Daily Life* (Albany: State University of New York Press, 1994).

Sylvia Walby, *Theorizing Patriarchy* (Oxford, UK: Basil Blackwell, 1990).

Rebecca Whisnant and Christine Stark, eds., *Not For Sale: Feminists Resisting Prostitution and Pornography* (North Melbourne, Australia: Spinifex Press, 2004).

INDEX

Index

If you would like to know more about Spinifex Press
write for a free complete 25-year catalogue or visit our website.

SPINIFEX PRESS
PO Box 212 North Melbourne
Victoria 3051 Australia
www.spinifexpress.com.au